The Practical Dog Listener

THE PRACTICAL DOG LISTENER

JAN FENNELL

HarperCollins*Publishers*

HarperCollins*Publishers*
77–85 Fulham Palace Road,
Hammersmith, London W6 8JB

www.**fire**and**water**.com

Published by HarperCollins*Publishers* 2002
1 3 5 7 9 8 6 4 2

Programme images reproduced by kind permission of
Channel 5 and Sunset and Vine Productions

A catalogue record for this book
is available from the British Library

ISBN 0 00 257205 2

Photography by Stephen Daniels

Set in Stempel Garamond

Printed and bound in Great Britain by
The Bath Press Ltd, Bath

For Sasha, Barmie and Raffie

CAUTION

It is important to state here that my method cannot remove the aggressive tendencies of any dog. Certain breeds have been raised specifically for the purpose of fighting, and my methods will never be able to alter their potentially savage nature. What my method can do is allow people to manage their dogs so that this aggressive instinct is never called upon. Please exercise the greatest of caution when working with such dogs.

CONTENTS

ACKNOWLEDGEMENTS

The process of producing this, my second book, was in many ways more difficult than the first. Once more, the fact that I have reached the finishing line is down to the professionalism and support extended to me by a special group of people.

First and foremost, I have to extend thanks to Val Hudson, Monica Chakraverty, Rachel Smyth and Jo Wilson at HarperCollins. Their guiding hands have been invaluable at every stage.

I am also grateful to John Leach, at Sunset & Vine, for providing stills from my television series, and photographer Stephen Daniels for his hard work in capturing elements of my method on film. Thanks, too, to Sadie, my German shepherd, for the patience she showed during that long and demanding photo session.

Nearer home, the people with whom I work on a day-to-day basis have remained rocks, my closest allies. To the names of my partner Glenn and son Tony, I can now add that of Ali Powrie, our very special new dog listener. Most of all, however, I would like to thank my agent Mary Pachnos. What began as a business acquaintance has evolved into a valued friendship. She is my trusted shield – I would be lost without her.

INTRODUCTION

The response to the publication of my first book, *The Dog Listener*, has been truly humbling. I seem to have struck a chord with so many people who share my belief that humans and dogs can enjoy a peaceful and rewarding coexistence. The thought that many of these people are now successfully implementing the compassionate training method I outlined, and so are learning to understand the dog's own language, heartens me enormously.

The many words of support I have received since publication echo those I first heard on a much smaller scale when I began treating problematic dogs almost ten years ago. At the time, people raised on the idea of 'obedience training', of sublimating the dog's will to that of its human 'master', were overwhelmed to discover that dogs could coexist with humans while still exercising their own free will. They were amazed to discover that, as I like to put it, the best form of control is using the dog's self-control.

People's responses to the practicalities of applying my method have conformed to an equally familiar pattern. And it was here that the seeds of the idea for this book were sown. From my earliest experiences in dealing with owners on a one-on-one basis, I quickly learned that no two dogs, no two homes and no two relationships between dog and owner are the same. On the one hand, this is one of the main reasons why my work remains such a source of fascination to me. However, this also makes it natural that my work divides itself into two distinct phases: the home visit itself and the post-visit, or backup, service.

During the crucial first consultation, it is my job to explain and demonstrate the principles that underpin my work. From there, I go on to offer owners basic instructions on how to implement my method. Many owners are able to replicate my method almost instantaneously, yet just as many require ongoing supervision. This is no criticism of any of them: while, at heart, my method is a simple one, the practicalities of implementing it are at times demanding. Some people don't have the time or the resources to devote themselves as fully as others. Some have tried so many different methods, they cannot separate mine from the others. Equally, while I believe all dogs understand and react to my signals in the same way, every dog has a personality that can manifest itself in a different form of behaviour. Some dogs are simply more strong-willed and resistant than others. As a result, I make sure I am always at the end of a telephone line to guide owners through the difficult moments.

My first book was, in many ways, the equivalent of the home visit. Within its pages I outlined my ideas and explained how they evolved through long and hard experience. It was, if you like, my mission statement. Now I have produced this second book as the backup, the practical guide to putting that philosophy to work. The reaction to the first book has helped shape the content of this companion volume. Many of the people who have contacted me since reading *The Dog Listener* have asked me to develop specific ideas touched on in the first book. Most of them have wanted to apply them to the practical realities of their own situations. Many people, for instance, own more than one dog. Others find it hard to impose themselves on their dog, to present the signals consistently and to interpret their dog's reaction correctly. Some find it difficult to incorporate my method into their hectic lives. Others have dogs that have displayed behaviour so bizarre, it simply hadn't occurred to me it existed! I have no doubt there are dogs out there with traits that I still haven't imagined. Nevertheless, I have done my best to cover as many of the unexplored areas as I can in this book.

My goal is to allow anyone to implement my method. So, to make it as accessible as possible, I have divided what follows into a guide through the key phases of the crucial first thirty days. I am adamant in my belief that the work of a responsible and caring owner begins even before a dog arrives within the home. With this in mind, I have included a section on the all-important preparations required too. From meeting and corresponding with people, I know how many readers enjoyed hearing of my adventures in treating problem dogs, so I have made sure I have included as many anecdotal examples as possible to illustrate my points. In response to readers' comments, there are also step-by-step photographs.

There are goals that can be achieved at regular intervals throughout this method. For instance, it is my belief that most dogs and their owners can attain a basic new understanding of each other within two days. Within a week, I believe most owners should be ready to begin taking their dogs out on walks in public places. At the same time, I am not so foolish as to claim that my method will turn even the most difficult and badly behaved dog into the perfect companion within a month. Nor am I going to promise that every dog's progress will conform to precisely the same pattern. If you find your dog is not doing something within four, fourteen – or even forty – days, you should not despair. Results will come with application and patience. Provided you persevere and apply my ideas consistently, even the most desperate owner should see huge improvements within this first month. Perhaps even more importantly, you should also have changed your perspective of your dog. Both of you should then be ready to join the growing band of owners and dogs that are enjoying a happier and more fulfilling life together.

Lincolnshire, England, October 2001

PROLOGUE

Home Truths

In the decade since I first began developing my ideas about communicating with dogs, I feel as if I've been travelling a long, mysterious – and seemingly endless – road. If I am honest, it has been a journey filled with more than its fair share of wrong turns and blind alleys. Yet around every corner there has been something new to learn.

My travels have now taken me far from home, and the close-knit community of friends and fellow dog lovers within which I began my work. It has been a privilege to meet and help – either directly or indirectly – dogs and owners as far afield as Thailand and the United States, New Zealand and France. Wherever I have travelled I have encountered situations that, sometimes subtly, sometimes dramatically, have deepened my understanding and reaffirmed my belief in the principles of the hidden language that underpins dog behaviour. It is ironic, then, that the most powerful and painful lesson of recent times should have been delivered within the confines of my own home.

There's an old saying that if you want to give God a laugh, you tell him your plans. It never seemed so apt as it did in May 2001. At the time, I must admit, I had been feeling on top of the world. I had travelled to Poland to promote the publication of my first book, *The Dog Listener*. It was the first time I had ventured abroad to talk about my work. Meeting dog lovers in cities like Warsaw, Lodz and Cracow was an exciting and uplifting experience, something I'd never imagined would happen to me. I was guest of honour at the country's main dog show and was fêted on television shows and at Champagne receptions and dinners; they treated me like royalty. On the plane back from Warsaw, I had much more to look forward to: a follow-up book, planning a series for television in the UK and finalising the details for my trip to New York, for the launch of the American edition of the book in late July – all heady stuff.

It wasn't long after I had set my suitcases down that I was brought crashing back to earth. God, it seemed, had got wind of my plans. At the time my partner, Glenn, and I shared our home in Lincolnshire with nine dogs. I'd set off to Poland knowing that the oldest of them, my eleven-year-old Jack Russell, Barmie, had been ill for some time. I wrote about Barmie in my previous book. I had come across him at an animal sanctuary where he had been brought after being discovered tied to a concrete block by a piece of rope. He had been horribly emaciated and was trembling: not just because it was winter at the time but also because he was utterly petrified of humans. I dread to think what sort of abuse he had suffered in his earlier life. The sanctuary was ready to put him to sleep because he was too nervous and aggressive to fit into a family home. I took him in and he became the first great test of my compassionate training method, then in its embryonic stage.

In the seven years I'd had him, Barmie had overcome his fear to lead a happy and fulfilled life. He was a bundle of good-natured energy. Unfortunately, because of the damage he'd suffered in his early years, he'd needed a great deal of medication. As he reached the autumn years of his life, it was clear the cumulative effect of the necessary steroids had weakened him. By that Spring his coat was bare – more skin than fur – his liver was enlarged and he was terribly weak. He was vomiting a lot: everything was breaking down. I'd been telling friends before my trip to Poland that I feared the worst. Sure enough, I got back to learn that he was in a pitiful state. I knew his time was at hand.

An even bigger bombshell lay ahead, however. Even before Barmie, my greatest insight into canine behaviour had been provided by Sasha, a beautiful, black German shepherd I had acquired as a puppy. I had begun my search for a new approach to communicating with dogs in 1990 after meeting the 'Horse Whisperer', Monty Roberts. Seeing him bring wild and untamed horses under control without resorting to force or violence of any kind had struck a profound chord within me. I had set out to find a way of training dogs in the same non-violent manner, communicating with the dog in its own language in the same way that Monty connected with horses. Sasha had come into my home soon afterwards and immediately proved an inspiration. More than any other of my dogs, Sasha had shown me the startling similarities between the leadership behaviour within the wolf pack and the domestic 'pack' of its distant relative, the dog. Without her guiding example, I would never have gained the knowledge I possess today.

Sasha was eight years old. She'd had problems with her waterworks about six weeks earlier, but a course of antibiotics seemed to cure her. About five days before I had flown to Poland the problem returned, only this time she was passing blood. The vet prescribed a stronger antibiotic and asked us to provide a urine sample so that he could work out the precise nature of her problem. When I got back from Poland, Glenn told me he had difficulty getting this from Sasha; she was having trouble passing water of any kind and her stomach had turned into a hard mass.

I had arrived back on a Thursday evening. On the Friday morning we had arranged to take Barmie to the vet. To be honest, I sensed the end was near. That morning he had been sick in the garden and had been unable to lift himself back to his feet after falling. When I described Sasha's condition to the vet, he told me to bring her along for an examination as well.

While one vet went off to examine Sasha, we went into one of the rooms with Barmie. It was clear now that he was in some pain. We took the decision to have him put to sleep. There are owners who can't bear to be present at this moment but, for me, it's so important that the last thing a dog sees is a friendly face, and that's what I provided for Barmie. At around noon on Friday, I sat there with him and cuddled him as the injection was administered. He was ready to go: he passed away within seconds.

On the way out, we spoke to the vet who was examining Sasha. The early prognosis seemed to be that she had a blockage, perhaps stones. I was so upset about Barmie I couldn't really think beyond that. I told them to do whatever was necessary, even if it meant operating. To be honest, I assumed the problem was treatable.

It was 3.30pm when the telephone rang again. The vet said: 'It's very bad news.' An x-ray had shown that there was no blockage. Further examination had shown that Sasha's bladder muscle had stopped working. He would do what he could to stimulate the bladder but he was not hopeful. I put the telephone down in a state of shock. I couldn't believe what was happening.

Rather than leaving Sasha in the clinic overnight, I brought her home. On Saturday morning I took her back to the vet and left her for more tests. At midday the phone rang again. Ominously, I was told that another vet had been brought in to provide a second opinion. At 2.30pm the phone rang again and a nurse told me that the vets had held a conference and agreed there was nothing that could be done. The nerve had been badly damaged somehow and, while it was possible to drain the bladder with a catheter, this was not something that could be done for any length of time. They could go ahead with exploratory operations but, in their opinion, this was not going to alter things. I was devastated. I remember telling the nurse: 'I want a miracle.' She seemed as upset as me. 'I wish we could give you one,' she replied gently.

For a while I considered letting the vets go ahead with their exploratory operations. But then I thought about Sasha, the noblest dog I have known, being reduced to this state. As far as I am concerned, there is no justification for prolonging a dog's life if it is in pain – regardless of how shocking and upsetting it is to the owner. My motto is simple: it's either them in pain or us in pain, and it should never be them. So it was that, for the second time in two days, Glenn and I drove to the clinic to have one of our beloved dogs put to sleep. We were both in a terrible state. When Sasha passed away, I cuddled her and simply said: 'Thank you.'

In the days that followed, I went through a whole range of emotions. Most of the time I felt sick inside. My head was spinning. My whole body hurt. I felt guilt and wondered whether I was being punished for something I had done. I felt anger that these dogs had been taken from me. I had wondered how I would be able to carry on with my work. In one of my few lighter moments, I even found myself agreeing with, of all people, the camp comedian Julian Clary. When he appeared on the BBC show *Room 101*, Clary – a dog lover – consigned the entire species to

'Room 101' because he said they didn't live long enough. 'They get under your skin and you love them and then they die,' he said. How true that is.

For all dog lovers, the loss of the creature they regard as their best friend is a devastating moment. Yet so many owners feel guilty or embarrassed or apologetic. They think they are being stupid. Over the years, I have heard many people say: 'I want to fall apart. I can't believe the way I am feeling.' I always tell them they are entitled to feel that way; their devastation is legitimate and natural. People who say, 'It was only a dog,' are the unlucky ones. They don't even begin to understand the love that a relationship with a dog can bring. Grief over the loss of a dog is as genuine as any other bereavement.

I was certainly not in the mood to apologise for feeling the way I did. Yet, in my heart, I knew I could not let these feelings overwhelm me for long. I soon realised I was not going to be allowed to.

When I got back from the vet and walked back into the house that afternoon, I felt like my world had collapsed. Hand on heart, I couldn't bear to see, let alone play with or cuddle, my remaining dogs. Dogs are such sensitive creatures, it was inevitable the pack would pick up on this. The remainder of my pack was made up of Sasha's daughter, Sadie, and six springer spaniels. These were Molly, aged five, and her children, Jake and Jen; Jen's one-year-old children, Reef and Opal; and another three-year-old springer, Ceri, and her two ten-week-old puppies, Todd and Gabby.

It was Sadie, perhaps predictably, who signalled her reaction first. While the others looked at me as normal when I came in, Sadie hung back. She kept her head hung low, as if she couldn't bear to catch my eye: I'm sure she sensed what had happened. To be honest, I couldn't bring myself to look at her either.

Tensions had been building within the house throughout the preceding few days. Sasha had been the most powerful personality within my canine pack. Her absence had thrown all the dogs out of kilter. We had already sensed an atmosphere and, before leaving for the vet that final time, had separated the dogs into four separate groups in different areas of the house.

By the time we arrived home it was late afternoon, almost feeding time. Glenn went through to the kitchen to organise the dogs' meal. We were both in such a state, however, that neither of us was thinking straight. And it was here that we made the sort of elementary mistake I spend my working life trying to prevent in other homes. We just released the dogs into the kitchen at the same time. Within a split second, all hell had broken loose.

Molly attacked Ceri in the most savage and direct way possible. She tore into her with a vengeance. Within another split second, Jen had joined in the fight on her mother's side. Even Sadie pitched into the mêlée. To see your dog being attacked by a stranger's animal is deeply distressing. To see your own dogs trying to tear each other to pieces was one of the most upsetting things I've seen in my life. It was a no-holds-barred confrontation. Wounds were opened and there was blood on the floor. The fact that neither Glenn nor I was badly bitten was more down to luck than judgement.

For a few brief seconds it was too much for me, I couldn't handle it. I can remember sobbing and screaming. At that moment I was confused and angry: how could they do this now? We had lost Sasha and all they could do was fight. It was only after we had pushed all the dogs into different areas of the house that my head began to clear and my senses returned.

It was not long before I recognised what had happened: it was blindingly obvious. For the last ten years I have developed my ideas about the dogs' belief in the hierarchical 'pack' system. I know, perhaps better than most, that a pack must – at all times – have a clearly defined chain of command and, in particular, a leader.

That afternoon, my dogs knew instinctively that there was something terribly wrong within the pack. It was worrying enough that the canine leader, Sasha, was not there. Even worse was the fact that the overall leaders, myself and Glenn, were effectively absent as well. The dogs had spent a few moments in our company before deciding we were about as convincing leaders as a couple of blancmanges. They knew that, for the pack to survive, its leadership had to be re-established immediately. The queen was dead, now it was a case of long live the queen. Molly's attack on Ceri was the opening salvo in the leadership battle. As the atmosphere calmed a little, I knew I had fallen into a trap. And I knew I had a monumental problem on my hands. It would take me weeks to even begin to reach a solution.

Naturally, the work I had to undergo to restore a sense of order and equilibrium within my pack will feature at intervals in the pages that follow. But I have chosen to begin with this story for another reason. In the days, weeks and months that followed those dreadful forty-eight hours, my anger slowly gave way to other emotions. I felt sorrow, bewilderment and a sense of loss. But, as things returned to something resembling normality, I felt a sense of gratitude too. It was a close friend who sowed the seed when she said to me: 'Those dogs were put here for a purpose. Sasha and Barmie have served that purpose, and now they have moved on.' She was absolutely right.

If it had not been for the inspiration Sasha and Barmie provided, I would not have known how to deal with the problems ahead, how to restore harmony to a family that had been left heartbroken by their parting. In time I realised that their legacy was going to live on. These two very different but equally lovable animals were the beacons that drove me on and made me believe it was possible to communicate with dogs.

In death – as in life – the two dogs were still showing me the way ahead. It was not simply that my remaining pack's instinctive, animal behaviour had confirmed all that Sasha and Barmie had first shown me. More importantly, as I thought about the events of that May, I saw something else: that communicating with our dogs is not a matter of cold, calculating science. Dogs, like humans, have powerful, and sensitive, personalities of their own. Our relationships with them are constantly changing, and we must be able to adapt with them. This was the challenge that faced me personally at that time. And it is a challenge that faces all dog owners, day in, day out. Again, this is something I hope to reflect in the pages to come.

It would, then, be impossible for me to continue this book without remembering – and thanking – Sasha and Barmie. These pages are the continuation of the work they first inspired. They may have gone from my arms but they have not gone from my heart.

PART ONE:

DAY -1

A Reintroduction to Dog Listening

When I saw my dogs attacking each other with such force after Sasha's death, I was witnessing a ritual that dates back thousands of years. It was around 12,000 BC that the modern dog, *Canis familiaris*, evolved from its ancient ancestor, *Canis lupus*, the wolf. In the centuries that have followed, the two animals have followed entirely different evolutionary paths. While the wolf has remained, to all intents and purposes, the same animal, the dog has multiplied into myriad breeds. While the wolf has remained in the wild, the dog has been domesticated. And while the wolf's life remains rooted within the same social environment – the pack – the modern dog has become integrated into human society, often living in isolation from other members of its species. On the surface, then, it may appear that the two have very little in common today. Nothing could be further from the truth.

At the beginning of the twenty-first century, our knowledge of our ancient *Homo sapiens* cousins deepens almost daily. Rather than fading with time, our understanding of their physiology and psychology seems to loom into focus more and more. And, as this happens, so science is growing increasingly certain that much of modern human behaviour remains rooted in this Stone-Age past. Many of our most basic instincts, from our mating rituals to our attitude to other tribes, date back to the cave-dwelling experience of our ancestors. When you think about it, this makes perfect sense. In the great scheme of things, we have existed on this planet for barely any time at all. If the lifetime of the earth is a single day, man's time on the planet amounts to barely a few minutes. Our circumstances and surroundings may have changed rapidly, but our brains – and therefore our fundamental natures – have hardly evolved from those times. If this is the case with humans, then it makes sense to assume it applies equally – if not even more strongly – to our closest companions in the animal world, dogs.

When the wolf, *Canis lupus*, integrated itself into human society, the two species formed a unique partnership. Their relationship was so special that burial chambers have been unearthed containing the skeletons of men and dogs buried alongside each other. Both were hunter-gatherers, both were communal. Both understood instinctively that survival was dependent on the power of the pack. Since then, this new strain of wolf, *Canis familiaris*, has evolved into a multitude of breeds. Just as the roots of the entire European population can supposedly be traced to seven women, so every dog – from the Pekinese to the Saluki, the Akita to the Alaskan husky – has a bloodline that leads back to the first domesticated dogs. At the same time, the remarkably close, instinctive relationship ancient man had with the dog has deteriorated and all but disappeared.

If we accept that *Canis familiaris'* basic programming remains much the same as it was when it first left its wolf-pack environment, it is not difficult to understand the forces that mould a modern dog's behaviour. The dog may have been taken out of the wolf pack, but the wolf pack can never be taken out of the dog.

To understand the way the modern dog views its world, we must therefore begin by looking at the society from which it first emerged and evolved: the wolf pack. For the wolf, the most powerful instincts are survival and reproduction. Driven by these instincts, the species has evolved a hierarchical system as strict and successful as any in the animal world. Every wolf pack is made up of leaders and subordinates, and at the head of every pack's pecking order are the ultimate rulers, the Alpha pair.

As the strongest, healthiest, most intelligent and most experienced members of the pack, it is the Alpha pair's job to ensure the pack's survival. As a result, they dominate and dictate everything the pack does, and their status is maintained by consistent displays of authority.

Underlining this, the Alpha pair are the only members of the pack who breed, thus ensuring only the healthiest genes survive. They are, in effect, twin dictators. They control and direct life within the pack, and the remainder of the pack accepts that rule unfailingly. Each subordinate member is content to know its place and function within this pecking order. Each lives happily in the knowledge that it has a vital role to play in the overall wellbeing of the pack.

The hierarchy of the pack is constantly reinforced through the use of highly ritualised behaviour. The ever-changing nature of pack life, in which Alphas and their subordinates are frequently killed or replaced through age, makes this essential. As far as the wolf's modern-day descendants are concerned, however, four main rituals hold the key to the pack instinct that lives on within them. They are central to my method.

THE FOUR RITUALS

1 The first key ritual is performed whenever a pack is reunited after being apart. As the pack reassembles, the Alpha pair remove any confusion by reasserting their dominance via clear signals to the rest of the pack. The pair have their own personal space, a comfort zone, within which they operate. No other wolf is allowed to encroach on this space unless invited to do so. By rejecting or accepting the attention of other members who wish to enter their space, the Alpha pair re-establish their primacy in the pack – without ever resorting to cruelty or violence.

2 When a kill has been made by the pack, the Alpha pair get absolute precedence when it comes to eating the carrion; the pack's survival depends on their remaining in peak physical condition. Only when they are satisfied and signal their feed is over will the rest of the pack be permitted to eat – and then according to the strict pecking order, with the senior subordinates feasting first and the juniors last. Back at the camp, the pups and 'babysitters' will be fed by the hunters regurgitating their food. The order is absolute and unbreakable. A wolf will act aggressively towards any animal that attempts to eat before it. Despite

the fact that the pack contains its blood relatives, an Alpha will attack any wolf that breaks with protocol and dares to jump the queue.

3 The Alpha pair repay the respect the pack bestows upon them with total responsibility for its welfare. Whenever danger threatens, it is the role of the Alpha pair to protect the pack. This is the third situation in which the natural order of the pack is underlined. The Alpha pair perform their leadership role unblinkingly, and from the front. They will react to danger in one of three ways, selecting one of the 'three Fs': flight, freeze or fight. Accordingly, they will run away, ignore the threat or defend themselves. Whichever response the Alpha pair select, the pack will again back up their leaders to the hilt.

4 Inevitably, the Alpha pair are at their most dominant during the hunt. Food, after all, represents the pack's most fundamental need; its very survival depends on it. As the strongest, most experienced and intelligent members of the pack, the Alpha pair take the lead during the search for new hunting grounds. When prey is spotted, they lead the chase and direct the kill. The Alphas' status as the pack's key decision-makers is never more in evidence than during this process. The wolf's prey can range from mice to buffalo. A pack may spend as long as four hours stalking, cornering and slaying its target. The logistics of this operation require a combination of organisation, determination, tactics and management skill. It is the Alpha's job to provide this leadership. It is the job of the subordinates to follow and provide support.

A Leap of Imagination

It is little wonder that so many people encounter problems in their relationship with their dogs. The vast majority of dog owners enter that relationship having made a series of utterly false assumptions. They have assumed, for instance, that the dog is in effect a child: an incapable, illogical – if deeply lovable – dependant. As a result of this, they have also assumed that it is going to respond to a series of childlike instructions issued in their language. They are viewing the dog and its world through the prism of the human experience: they are wrong.

The dog does not understand or relate to the human experience in any way. The fact that it responds to the word 'sit' or 'come' after hearing it a thousand times does not mean that it understands the spoken human language. It has simply come to associate these sounds with certain forms of behaviour, and has learned to act accordingly.

To lead a happy and fulfilling life with dogs, all owners need to make a fundamental change in their approach. They need to look at the world from the dog's perspective, and understand the society and the rules under which the dog believes it is living. A leap of the imagination is required. They need to understand that the dog is not an immature child operating within the human world: it is an intelligent adult operating within the structures and strictures of its own highly regulated society: the pack. And, most importantly of all, the dog believes it has been given the job of leading that pack. Viewed from this perspective, all its behaviour will make sense. And, viewed from this perspective, all owners have the opportunity to forge a new and hugely fulfilling relationship with their dog.

Amichien Bonding

A dog believes it is a functioning member of a community that operates according to principles directly descended from the wolf pack. Whether its 'pack' consists of itself and its owner, or a large family of humans and other animals, the dog believes it is part of a social grouping and a pecking order that must be adhered to at all times. What is more, all dogs believe they are the elected leader of that pack. And they believe this because the humans with whom they live send out signals that re-elect them to the role on a daily basis.

It is my belief that all of the problems we encounter with our dogs are rooted in their belief that they rather than us, their owners, are the leaders of their particular packs. It is the correction of this misconception that lies at the heart of the communications technique I have developed, called Amichien Bonding.

Four separate elements make up the bonding process. Each correlates to the specific times I have identified when the pack's hierarchy is established and underlined. On each occasion, the dog is confronted with a question that we must answer on its behalf by providing clear, concise signals that it will understand. The four occasions are:

- **When the pack reunites after a separation, who is the boss now?**
- **When the pack eats food, what order do we eat in?**
- **When the pack is under attack or there is a fear of danger, who is going to protect us?**
- **When the pack goes on the hunt, who is going to lead us?**

Each set of signals will be introduced individually with the 'hunt', or walk, tackled last of all. It will eventually be necessary for you to use all four elements in conjunction with each other. Your dog must, in effect, be blitzed with signals. It needs to learn that it is not its responsibility to look after you, that it is not its job to care for the house, that all it has to do is sit back and lead a comfortable and enjoyable life. It is a mantra that must be repeated over and over again. Only then will your dog get the message that it is no longer in charge, only then will it be able to exercise the most powerful form of control, self-control.

The process is, at heart, a simple one. The most powerful central principles are established within the first few hours of application. From there, you will go on to add additional signals and controls, first within the home, then within the outside world. By the end of the first thirty days, you should have laid the foundations for a lifetime of companionship and co-operation. What follows is a guide to these formative, first thirty days.

In many ways, the process that is about to begin is akin to a revolution. The objective will be to stage a bloodless coup, to remove the leadership from the dog, but to do so without resorting to force or violence in any way. No coup in history has succeeded without precise and careful planning. And this one will be no exception…

TO BE OR NOT TO BE A DOG OWNER

'There is no faith which has never yet been broken, except that of a truly faithful dog.'

Konrad Lorenz

It is no surprise to me that dogs have for centuries remained the inspiration for words like these. The love, loyalty and companionship that a dog can bring into our lives are unique. And, in theory, they are pleasures that everyone should have the right to enjoy. I write 'in theory' because I do not, in all honesty, believe it is a right that should be granted automatically. It is a sad fact of life that there are people who take dogs into their home for all the wrong reasons. The animal sanctuaries and dogs' homes of the world are filled with the unhappy results of their rash and unthinking behaviour.

It has become a cliché to say that a dog is not for Christmas, it is for life. But it remains true nevertheless. A dog brings with it a set of responsibilities. And no one should take on the task of introducing a dog into their home without weighing up whether they are ready, willing and able to live up to these responsibilities.

There have probably been thousands of books written on the pros and cons of taking on a dog. I do not intend to contribute another one. Having said that, I do have some opinions on the matter. Anyone who is only getting a dog for their children to play with should not get a dog. Dogs and young people can forge the most beautiful relationships of all – but only if the child is taught to respect the dog: they are not toys. Anyone who is getting a dog solely for the purpose of guarding their homes should not get a dog: this is not fair. Anyone who intends getting a dog and then leaving it at home all day should think again, or should make appropriate arrangements for a friend or professional walker to take it out. The dog is a social animal and, if it is cut off from other beings for eight to twelve hours, this is not good for it.

I also believe that all owners must prepare themselves for the reality of dog ownership. It is the easiest job in the world when the dog is a lovable ball of fluff and affection, but what about when it falls ill or misbehaves, fouls the living-room carpet or growls at visitors? And what about heading out into the outside world? Are you prepared to head out on cold, inhospitable winter mornings to walk the dog? Are you willing to become a fully paid-up member of the plastic-bag brigade and clean up after your dog in public? And what about the time it falls ill and you face the potentially astronomical vet's bills?

Of course, good owners – rather like good parents – think about a lot of these things instinctively. But I would ask even these genuine dog lovers to do a little soul-searching before committing themselves to using my method. It is one thing to understand the challenges of my approach from the human point of view, but what about thinking about this from the dog's perspective? Dogs are living, breathing creatures with needs and feelings of their own. No one would welcome a deaf person into their family without accepting in advance that they would need to learn some form of sign language. It is no different with a dog. So, for this reason, I would ask you to consider the following:

- **Are you prepared to go into this with an open mind?**
- **Are you willing to forget and discard all other 'training' methods?**
- **Are you prepared to accept the dog's welfare is paramount?**
- **Are you prepared to work hard and make the sacrifices necessary to understand a language that may prove elusive and confusing at times?**
- **Are you prepared to give the time the dog needs, especially during the early stages when patience and perseverance are of primary importance?**
- **Has the whole family discussed what is going to be required?**
- **If you already own dogs, are you prepared to go through the necessary retraining they will need as well?**

These are all tough questions. I make no apologies for posing them, however. I much prefer that people understand their dogs before they learn to love them. I would rather they begin knowing that sacrifices and hard work will be required. Yet, if my years of experience have taught me anything, it is that the effort is far, far outweighed by the rewards that come from having a happy, well-adjusted and relaxed dog.

WHERE TO GET A DOG

To my mind, there are only two sources from which we should buy dogs: respectable, responsible breeders and registered rescue centres or dogs' homes. There is, I know, a wide range of alternative sources, from pet shops to so-called licensed kennels. Yet I would not recommend that a dog be taken from any of these, for the following two reasons.

Firstly, it is my firm belief that, if at all possible, an owner should be able to see the dog's mother and gain knowledge of the history of both parents before taking the dog away. This is something I will explain in more detail in a moment. Secondly, it is only through the first two sources that an owner will have any comeback.

As an illustration of this latter point, I often use the example of a close friend of mine, Wendy Broughton. Wendy is a keen horsewoman. It was Wendy who introduced me to Monty Roberts, the Horse Whisperer, from whom I learnt so much. At a horse fair one day, Wendy saw a batch of dogs for sale for £15 each. There were no clues as to where these dogs had come from. Their owners that day had only one interest: making money. Wendy is a soft touch and took pity on one dog in particular. In the two years since then, she has spent more than £2500 on vet's bills. It turned out the dog was riddled with worms and suffered from a variety of stomach problems.

The crucial point here is that Wendy had no comeback on the people who sold her that dog; she didn't even get a contact name. This type of trade is sadly on the increase. The growth of 'puppy farms' is something I abhor. Often, owners will be allowed no more than seventy-two hours in which to return their dogs.

In contrast, no reputable breeder or rescue centre would sell a dog without guaranteeing that you could return the animal to them if there were a medical problem or if you were, for whatever reason, unhappy with it. Indeed, a good breeder would insist on being on hand to provide advice throughout the dog's days. The dog cannot lose under this arrangement: if it fits into a happy home, it will enjoy a long and hopefully rewarding life there. If not, it will return to a place where its best interests are safeguarded. Owners who leave themselves with no comeback, are left with no obvious place to return an unwanted dog. Many will, of course, ensure they are given good homes. Sadly, many more will not.

Buying a Puppy

Falling in love with a puppy is the easiest thing in the world. We've all experienced the 'aaah' factor, that moment when we've stared for the first time into the saucer-sized eyes of a sweet, young dog and gone hopelessly gooey. It's for this reason that I recommend you begin your search for a puppy by steering clear of these charmers to begin with. You know that you are going to fall head over heels in love with the puppy – it's a given. Far better for you to deal with the realities before beginning the romance, and the best way to do this is by first meeting the family.

Producing a litter of puppies involves collaboration between the human breeder and their dogs. The dogs deliver this new life into the world, but it is the human who must shoulder the ultimate responsibility. I passionately believe that the best way to assess whether a dog is coming from a good home is by meeting both sets of 'parents', that is both the human and canine carers.

Given that many breeders go to a stud to begin their litters, it is more than likely that only the mother will be available. The condition of the owner and its home, its personality, temperament and general demeanour will reveal much. Of course, part of the equation is missing if the father is not there. Seeing both will provide the clearest idea possible of the sort of dog their offspring is going to become, nevertheless, a visit to the mother will always be worthwhile.

Just as importantly, the attitude and behaviour of the owner is highly revealing too. If, for instance, the mother is not with its puppies, there are immediate reasons for concern. The growth of puppy farms is one of the more unpleasant facts of life these days. The absence of the mother may mean that the seller is a third party, whose motives are purely to do with money rather than the welfare of the dogs in their protection.

Another good indicator of the quality of the home is the extent to which the seller interrogates all potential new owners. A potential buyer should expect to be grilled by a good breeder: I know, as I always insist on finding out as much as I can about anyone who wants to take one of my puppies into their home. The procedure should be like that of an adoption society being very careful about where it places the children entrusted to its care. Good breeders should be just as diligent in finding a home for the innocent young lives for which they are responsible.

A reputable breeder should want to know everything about the home into which they are considering releasing the puppy. They should want to know what the domestic situation is at home: are there people around all day to look after the dog? Are there many small children in the home? Has the prospective owner owned this type of dog, or indeed any dog, before? Another important question is whether the prospective owner has thought about whether a particular breed is right for their home. Also, are they willing to wait for a puppy? Good breeders do not churn out dogs as if from a production line. If the breeder asks these questions, it should be seen as a positive sign. If they do not, they are probably more interested in making a sale and should therefore be treated with caution.

By the same token, a good breeder should be open to questions from a potential owner. They should be willing to reveal anything and everything about the dog's history and background, from the details of its parentage and its age, to its favourite food and toys. Again, owners should be wary of anyone who is vague or unhappy about answering these questions. I've never been afraid to talk to potential owners in this kind of detail. Indeed, I've made very good friends of people who have bought puppies from me.

Potential owners should be particularly careful about checking for hereditary problems within some breeds. Cavalier King Charles spaniels can be prone to heart problems, for instance; Dalmatians can suffer from deafness; long-backed breeds, like basset hounds and dachshunds, have a tendency to suffer from back pain and slipped discs. With German shepherds and Labradors, potential buyers should look out for hip dysplasia, a genetic problem in which the ball-and-socket joint of the hip can be deformed or even nonexistent. It is a condition that is extremely painful and ultimately crippling for dogs that are afflicted and something that good breeders monitor closely. Dogs are x-rayed at the age of one and given a 'hip score', which ranges from zero for perfect hips, to eighteen and higher, a mark that indicates the dog should not be used for breeding.

All good breeders work hard to eliminate these problems. But, so as to make informed and appropriate choices, potential owners are well advised to thoroughly research the breeds they are interested in. This is easily done through the Kennel Club or its equivalent organisation, and then through the various breed experts. The importance of this cannot be overstressed. No one goes out to make a major purchase like a new car or a house without checking out the subject thoroughly. When they choose a dog, owners are introducing into the family a new member that will hopefully remain with them for twelve to fourteen years; it is not something to be taken lightly.

Rescue Dogs

Few things can compare with the pleasure that comes from providing a home for a rescue dog – that is, a dog that has been placed in a sanctuary or dogs' home due to abuse, abandonment or bad behaviour. As someone who has taken in a number of rescue dogs over the years, I can say with my hand on my heart that the rewards both the dogs and I have had have been phenomenal. The joy I have had in seeing tragic dogs given a new hope in life has been immense. And I have to admit it has made me feel good to have provided these dogs with a happy and stable home life they had previously been denied.

Having said that, there is no escaping the fact that rescue dogs can present considerable problems, for self-evident reasons. I often say that there is no such thing as a problem dog, but there are dogs with problems. And rescue dogs, by their very nature, come with more problems than most.

Obviously in such cases it is simply not possible to make the checks that are possible with a new puppy. Any decent sanctuary or rescue organisation should be able to provide you with some details about the dog's immediate past. Again, vagueness or reluctance to give out details should be regarded with extreme caution, however, the vast majority of sanctuaries and rescue homes are run by people who have an extraordinary dedication to dogs and their welfare. Whatever they know about the dog, they will be willing to tell you: good or bad. It is not in their interest, or that of the dog, to deceive you. The reason many dogs are in a sanctuary is due to violence. I believe, however, that, provided you understand the way a dog's mind works, it is a calculated risk. For many people, I hope it will remain a risk worth taking.

A Question of Breeding

When I was given my first dog, a Border collie called Shane, there were relatively few breeds readily available to buy. How things have changed. Today, new owners face a bewildering choice of breeds, from exotic Oriental dogs like the Akita and the shih-tzu, to breeds that, until recently, were considered rare, like the Newfoundland or husky.

I am often asked whether particular breeds are more suitable for some people than others. My answer, in general, is that anyone can own any breed provided the dog fully understands its status within the domestic pack. A Yorkshire terrier that believes it is boss may not deliver as bad a bite as a Rottweiler or German shepherd under the same delusion; nonetheless, a bite is a bite. If a dog's attitude is right, this problem will not arise so the breed of dog is immaterial, yet there are some general guidelines you should bear in mind.

If, for instance, you have a quiet, family lifestyle and are looking for a more relaxed companion rather than an active dog, you might be advised to take a breed that does not need as much exercise, something like a Tibetan spaniel. This does not necessarily mean a smaller dog: Great Danes and Saint Bernards love to lie around. On the other hand, people, like me, who find it hard to justify going out for a walk without a dog for company, are spoilt for choice. German shepherds, Labradors, springer spaniels are all suitable companions.

You have to bear in mind the specifics of your situation. For example, I would not advise someone who is restricted in what they are able to do physically to take on dogs with heavy coats, breeds like the Afghan hound or rough collies. The demands these breeds make in terms of grooming are considerable. It is far better for people in this situation to go for a Labrador, a retriever or a Border collie, dogs that are less 'high maintenance' in this respect.

You should also bear in mind the practicalities of training a dog. For instance, with the introduction of basic controls such as the 'sit' and 'heel', you will be required to do a lot of crouching and bending down to deal with your dog. Older, less mobile, people might want to bear in mind whether they are going to be capable of doing this with a small dog in particular. It is a lot easier to reach the eye level of a German shepherd than that of a lhasa apso.

It is worth stating at this point that it is wrong to associate the size of the dog with the size of the task ahead of its new owner. Big dogs do not necessarily mean a bigger task in terms of training and maintaining them. Indeed, in my experience, some of the kindest, gentlest and easiest-trained dogs have been from the larger breeds. And some of the most unco-operative have been from the smaller ones.

Of course, the best way to understand the type of dog you are acquiring is to study the breed. Each breed was originally evolved, through human intervention, to perform certain functions. Border collies and German shepherds were bred as sheepdogs, and are carers and herders. Beagles were bred to hunt. The Saint Bernard and the Newfoundland were bred as rescue dogs – it is why, in normal circumstances, they are such peaceful, placid dogs. It is only when an emergency arises that they leap into action. By the same token, lhasa apsos and

Pekinese were bred as lapdogs. Breeds like this are, literally, custom-made for people who are looking for warmth, affection and companionship above all else. There are dogs to suit everyone.

The one thing I would caution against is getting a dog purely because it is in vogue at a particular time. Certain breeds come into fashion every now and again. I can recall times here in Britain when the Afghan hound and the Old English sheepdog became incredibly 'trendy' dogs. The success of the film *101 Dalmatians* suddenly made that breed popular. A short time later, when these breeds are no longer *de rigueur*, the sanctuaries and rescue centres are full of unwanted dogs. In the mean-time, unscrupulous breeders will have gone into overtime producing as many puppies as possible, inflicting God-knows-what damage on the breed itself. If someone is going to choose an accessory from a fashion magazine, let it be a handbag, a pair of shoes or a dress – anything but a dog.

EXPANDING PACKS:
PREPARING FOR A NEW DOG

The more I have observed and worked with humans and dogs, the more I have come to recognise our shared sense of family values. It is, of course, no accident that dogs possess a pack instinct as deep-rooted as our own. It is one of the reasons why our ancient ancestors forged an alliance with the dog, the first and most important animal to be domesticated by man. I mention it at this point because you must consider this when you expand your pack by introducing new dogs to a home that already has dogs. My method, as I have explained, allows you to position yourself as the leader of that pack. Yet, in situations where you already own two or more dogs, the dogs, too, will have a hierarchy. The natural result when a new dog is introduced into the pack is a situation where the dogs believe a leadership election is about to happen. I will deal in detail with this later on, but for now bear in mind that the introduction of a new dog is something that has to be planned with particular care.

There are many other factors to consider. Mixing breeds, for instance, has to be thought about. A Japanese Akita and a German shepherd will get along together eventually, but there may be a great deal of friction before they settle into a routine together. Introducing a puppy less than nine months old to an existing pack is, in relative terms, a straightforward process. But here, too, you must bear in mind that placing a nine-month-old puppy in a home is the equivalent, in dog years, of introducing a hyperactive twelve-year-old to a human household. People always talk of one dog year being the equivalent of seven human years: in the case of the dog's first year, however, this is more like sixteen years. Look at it this way: by nine months old, a bitch is physically capable of producing and raising children. Emotionally, however, she is nowhere near ready. You should always bear in mind the effect a newcomer like this might have on the chemistry of your existing pack.

If you already have dogs, I therefore suggest you do two things before expanding the pack. Firstly, I recommend you introduce my method to the existing dogs first. This makes obvious sense on every level: the influence the existing dogs have on their new companion will be immense. If they have learned to live a fulfilling life by accepting you as their leader, the chances of the potentially disruptive newcomer accepting the status quo are hugely increased.

Secondly, I also advise you to introduce the new dog to its prospective pack as soon as possible. The ideal option is to take the existing dogs to the breeder or rescue centre where the new dog is. This has several obvious advantages. In territorial terms, it is neutral ground. The new arrival will also be amongst people who know and can control it in the event of problems. Most importantly of all, if after a few meetings there is clearly a high degree of friction between the old and new dogs, you will have the chance to think again. Once more, you will be able to get a strong idea of whether a refuge is a reputable one or not from their handling of this whole process. Alarm bells should begin ringing if they are reluctant to allow you to bring your dogs to meet the potential family member. The danger signals become overwhelming if the refuge even hints at the sale being cut and dried.

PREPARING THE HOME

A dog does not really care whether its owner lives in a tent or a palace. The criteria it regards as important are more to do with the comfort, safety and quality of life it enjoys rather than the particulars of its surroundings. If only we humans were less materialistic sometimes: as long as a dog is cared for in the right way, it will be happy.

In preparing to put my method into practice, I would advise you to make a few specific provisions around the home. Some of them are obvious, others less so. Each is important if life with a new dog is to get off on the right footing.

Sleeping Quarters

Decide where the dog is going to sleep. It is vital that the dog or puppy has its own space, its own refuge. It must be able to lie down on its side with about three to four inches to spare either side. It should have about the same space when it stretches out lengthwise. I personally like to use dog cages: my dogs seem to enjoy the idea that they have their own secure, enclosed space. I always leave the gate open so they can move freely. They are also perfect for travelling in the car.

A dog does not need to have an expensive basket or kennel of its own; a supermarket cardboard box turned on its side provides a safe, secure space. I always find putting an old jumper in it helps. It provides warmth and cover but has the added advantage over a clean blanket that it also smells of the family.

No-Go Areas

Decide on the no-go areas in the home. There will be areas where you will not want the dog to stray, typically bathrooms and toilets,

Open cages provide a cosy, secure and fun living space.

maybe a study or dining room. You should establish these areas in your mind in advance. Every member of the family should also be aware of the rules: instilling them into the dog will prove that much easier later on.

Gates: With the above in mind, I recommend placing a children's gate between the kitchen and the hallway. It ensures that the dog does not follow you everywhere, something that is a particular trait with puppies. At the same time, you will be able to keep an eye on the dog's movements. The only thing to watch out for is that the gaps between the bars are not wide enough for the dog to get its head stuck.

Garden: The garden area will be of vital importance to both you and your dog, not just during the first thirty days but also throughout your lives together. You should ensure that the area is secure and that your dog cannot escape. As with the internal gates, you should also make sure there is no danger of the dog's head being trapped in fencing. In assessing this, I do warn owners that I have had to extricate puppies from the most unlikely places: don't underestimate their ability to stick their heads in the tightest spaces!

Basic Needs

It may be stating the blindingly obvious here, but there are still many owners who seem to overlook the most basic practical preparations for the arrival of a new dog. The list that follows is customised to allow you to apply my method immediately.

Feeding Bowls: Two bowls are essential. One is for water, which should be filled with fresh water twenty-four hours a day and should be changed at least two to three times a day. The other is for food. As you will see later, an extra supply of bowls – up to four per dog – may come in useful in applying part of my method.

Collar and Lead: It will be several days before the dog is ready to go on a walk. Before then, however, there will be times when it will be used for heel work inside the house.

Toys: Again, there is no need to go to any extraordinary expense here. For puppies in particular, I find there is nothing better than an old tea towel or blanket, soaked in water, then tied in a knot. It is perfect for young dogs with immature, malleable teeth.

Grooming Brushes: Grooming is an important element of looking after a dog. As well as keeping the dog in condition, it allows you to keep a regular monitor on your animal's weight, skin condition and general welfare. It is also another means of forging a close personal bond with a dog. Long-haired dogs like cocker spaniels and Old English sheepdogs cannot be left for more than six days without being brushed. The knotted coat that results after this time can be painful and extremely unhygienic. Owners will need a 'slicker' brush for these dogs. For smooth-coated dogs, a soft brush will suffice. I also find it useful to use a pair of rubber gloves. They can be perfect for scrubbing particularly tricky areas clean.

First-Aid Kit: In case of emergencies, it is advisable to have a collection of medicines, such things as wound dressings, ointments and ear drops.

Food Rewards: An essential element of the work that lies ahead involves the awarding of tidbits of food. Before your dog arrives, ensure there is a good supply of special treats, things such as reward sticks, meat strips or (my personal favourite) pieces of cheese.

Good, Local Vet: I suggest to all potential dog owners that they spend a little time checking out the vets in their area. It is a good idea to get the dog registered in advance.

MENTAL PREPARATION

By far the most important preparation is that which must go on in your head. Unless you have grasped the central principles of my method, you should not proceed with it. You must be ready to see every situation in the right context: in terms of the dog and its view of its place in the domestic 'pack'. In addition, you must also make practical preparations for the days ahead.

Never Set Yourself Up for Failure
One important piece of advice I like to get across to owners from the

start is that they should never set themselves up for failure. By this I mean that, in the days ahead, there will be some setbacks that you cannot predict – and they are probably going to be related to the particular traits of your dog's personality. But, at the same time, there are going to be some mistakes that you can avoid through proper, careful planning, for instance, you should always have a ready supply of food reward with you. Try to be prepared for every eventuality that is thrown at you.

Allow More Time

Absolutely central to everything I do is a sense of calm. For this reason, you must be prepared to allow more time for everything; if you are impatient, it won't happen. You must be ready to put your dog's needs high on your agenda for a month. You must be ready to put yourself out for your dog. And, throughout this time, you must remember that you are taking into your home a creature whose language and needs are different from yours. Most crucial of all, you must accept that the dog is not going to learn your language – it is up to you to learn the dog's language. And, for this reason, every grown-up member of the family must take some time to familiarise themselves with the principles of bonding before the process begins.

Think Canine

A good owner should always anticipate their dog's doubts and questions. You should try to think ahead and recognise the things that a dog is going to find confusing or frightening. For instance, a dog is not being stupid if it recoils when a vacuum cleaner or a dishwasher or washing machine is switched on. I ask people to imagine how they would feel if they didn't comprehend what they were encountering. They'd want to know whether this was some-thing that was going to cause them harm.

Be Ready, Willing and Mentally Able

Learning my method is akin to learning a new language. Anyone who has had to master this skill will know what a difficult and time-consuming business it can be. They will also know that it requires absolute concentration and commitment, and a mind that is receptive and open to new ideas. It is no different with my method: you must not only be willing and able to learn, you must be mentally ready too. This is why I do not recommend you begin at times of emotional stress. Far better to postpone the introduction of Amichien Bonding until your mind is clear and focused.

I myself was reminded of the importance of mental preparation in the aftermath of the loss of Sasha and Barmie. Their deaths – and the explosive reaction it sparked within my own pack – left me reeling for days. Throughout that time, I knew that I would have to reintroduce all the elements of my method, that I would have to re-establish myself as the unchallenged leader of the pack. The reality was that I was nowhere near ready to do so at that time. My mind was filled with memories of dogs that I had loved and lost over the years. I was in a dream, or nightmare, for most of the next few days. I was angry, hurt and lost.

I was experienced enough by then to know that there was no point in my trying to reapply my method while I was in that state of mind. For the first few days after the fight took place, I simply kept the different factions within my pack separate at all times. I knew how unconvincing I was as a leader. I was being consumed by my human side, there was no place for thinking in the canine terms I needed: it simply would have failed. And I was not going to set myself up for a failure. No one reading this book should take the next step on this journey without being sure they too are willing, able and mentally ready to do so.

PART TWO

THE FIRST 48 HOURS

New Horizons:
Settling a New Dog in Its Environment

The road ahead is a long, sometimes difficult, but hopefully richly rewarding one. And for some owners, the first potential wrong turn looms within the first moments of bringing a dog home. Dogs that are already acclimatised and settled into a home will be able to begin the first phase of my method – reuniting after separation – immediately. For dogs that are new arrivals, whether they be puppies, adults or rescue dogs, there is a preliminary hurdle to be overcome. It is vital if the new relationship is to get off to the correct start.

Most of us can vividly recall moments like our first day at school, or our arrival at our first workplace. It is an extremely stressful, daunting and, at times, downright terrifying experience. People are operating according to a set of rules we don't yet understand. The place is filled with unfamiliar sights, sounds and smells. Imagine someone having to fit into a new environment like this when nobody understands what they are saying. This is the situation a dog faces when it takes its first tentative steps into a new home.

Arriving in a new environment is a traumatic experience for a dog. The most important thing you can do during the first forty-eight hours or so is to make this as trauma-free as possible. And it is imperative that the first minutes of the day are spent allowing the dog to settle into its new environment.

The first thing I recommend you do with a new dog or puppy is that, on arrival at the new home, you immediately take it outside to do its toiletting. When the dog relieves itself as you have asked it to, you should reward it with a tidbit. This should be accompanied with warm words of encouragement, such as 'Good dog', or 'Clean dog', and perhaps a stroke of the head or nape of the neck area. The key point here is that the first piece of positive association has been achieved within the first few moments in the home. A good start has been made.

The next stage is to allow the dog to get to know its new environment. You should leave it alone and let it explore the areas it is free to roam in. Throughout this time, you should be giving out gently affectionate signs, by which I mean smiles and words of reassurance and kindness. At the same time, you should not be gushing or overaffectionate with the dog. This is particularly important in the case of rescue dogs. These are dogs that have had appalling experiences in the outside world. For understandable reasons, their trust may be much harder to win. The key thing here is to remain kind and calm but to keep a respectful distance too. It may well be that the dog is too nervous to engage in any way during the first few hours, or even days. Do not rush the dog: give it space and time.

Settling a dog down into a new environment may sound straightforward. It is not, I can assure you. As an illustration of the hard work that is sometimes required here, I often draw on the example of Murphy. All dogs need to check out their new home, to sniff out the landscape, if you like. Murphy was more qualified than most for this job. He was a police 'sniffer' dog. At work, his role was to locate drugs, explosives and contraband.

I met him while visiting his handler, Teresa, a PC with the West Midlands Police. She had expressed an interest in learning more about my method and I had visited her at her home. Murphy, I discovered, lived in a kennel at the rear of the house. When I wondered why he didn't live in the house she simply laughed: 'He'd destroy the place,' she said. By this, she meant that Murphy was simply too inquisitive. His training had encouraged him to stick his nose in anywhere and into anything suspicious. On the rare occasions he had been allowed in people's homes, this had led to disaster. He would knock things over and generally leave a trail of destruction behind him. In short, he had no house manners.

I offered to illustrate my work by introducing Murphy to the house. He immediately went berserk, leaping around everywhere. I immediately asked for his lead. While Teresa and I sat down and talked, we studiously ignored Murphy's high-octane behaviour. Throughout, he remained attached to his lead, which Teresa clung to from her chair. After ten minutes or so, he settled down. At this point, Teresa released him from his lead. The reprieve was short-lived: the moment he began leaping around again, I got Teresa to put him back on his lead. She didn't scold him or shout at him. She simply remained aloof and acted quickly. This process was repeated four times in all.

The next time Murphy was let off the lead, he simply sniffed around our legs. It was as if he was making his final check of the environment. Soon after that, he lay nicely down at Teresa's side. It was the final symbolic gesture, the signal that he was now ready to begin living, and learning, there.

It is no surprise that many people have problems integrating new dogs into a home that already has one or more dogs living there. My method will ensure that the human members are elevated to the senior positions within the extended pack, but it is important that you acknowledge the canine pecking order below this. This hierarchy is the most natural thing in the world, and nothing is going to change that.

In many, many cases dogs settle into a natural order with very little trouble indeed. But, make no mistake about it, the process can be hugely competitive and can result in aggressive and potentially violent behaviour. For this reason, I must emphasise how essential it is that the initial, introductory meeting between dogs happens on neutral territory. In an ideal world, I would recommend more than one meeting.

If, for whatever reason, your existing pack is only going to meet the new dog on the day of its arrival, this introduction must be your first task of the day. You must choose a neutral ground, and here you must be careful to avoid places where the existing pack has strong associations. In the past, I have taken new additions to my pack to parks or open spaces, areas where they and my existing dogs have been free to weigh each other up and begin the process of integration in a less charged atmosphere. It requires the assistance of someone else to lead either the existing pack or the newcomer to the spot. Even if this only lasts for half an hour before the new dog arrives home, it can be of huge long-term benefit.

If there is more than one dog in the existing pack, I suggest you introduce these dogs to the newcomer one at a time. Each time this happens, it is vital the two dogs meet on equal status. As the newcomer is going to be on a lead, the existing pack member should also be on a lead. If one dog is being rewarded with toys or treats, then so should the other. The vital thing here is that the two dogs form a new, extended pack. By exuding strong leadership, you should be implanting the idea that the job of Alpha within this pack is already taken. The newcomer will obviously be less well versed in your communication methods than the established dog. Yet the message should begin to seep through just the same: by all means sort out a pecking order amongst yourselves, but be certain that the job of leader is not up for grabs – nor will it ever be.

As you allow the dogs to get to know each other, the key message here is 'don't panic'. If the dogs grumble or growl at each other, ignore it until they relax. Ultimately, dogs enjoy each other's company. Given time and space, a friendship can emerge from the least likely pairing. Throughout this period, it is again important to show the qualities of leadership at all times. So everything should remain calm, and you should keep your head.

It is worth stating that you should adopt a sensible approach towards aggression between dogs here. I have seen people overreact completely to the sight of two dogs squaring up to each other and growling. In human terms, this is no more serious than one person telling another to get out of their sight. It is not the most pleasant situation, but neither is it an excuse for the sort of histrionics I have witnessed in my time. If your dogs do threaten each other, you should act decisively and immediately to remove the instigator. For this reason, I would recommend that the new dog wears a collar while it is being introduced to the pack: it is better to be safe than sorry.

Once a rapport is established, let the dogs move closer together. Eventually, they should come up close enough so that they can play together. This is the most natural thing in the world. Again, remain relaxed and let it happen naturally. The more time the new extended pack spends together in this way, the better. Eventually, however, they will have to head home. The dogs should be transported home together. If the established dog is being reluctant getting into a vehicle, you should put the new dog in first. If the situation becomes tense or confrontational during the journey, the new dog should be moved to another seat. Once at home, the dogs must remain on equal status, each of them on a lead. They should be released in the garden at the same time and, while you keep an eagle eye on them, they should then be left to get to know each other.

There is every chance, of course, that the dogs will not get on immediately. You will have to exercise common sense and flexibility here. I strongly recommend that you should make plans for segregating your dogs at home in the early days. Dogs are quick to assimilate themselves into environments: in most instances, I believe dogs can settle into a new home within forty-eight hours. Yet, given the potentially explosive situation that can arise when a dog is added to an established pack, I ask people to be overcautious. I have certainly found that providing both the newcomer and existing dogs with their own 'bolt holes' can prove an invaluable asset in the testing early days.

It is vital that your new dog is allowed to stake out its environment, so, if you are lucky enough to have the space, I recommend you build a separate area – a compound, if you will – in which the new dog can begin its life within the home. It should be given all the time it needs to assimilate to this space. At the same time, use the separate 'neutral' area for your existing dogs to continue to get to know the stranger now in their midst – always under close supervision by you. The length of time the extended pack spends together should be increased slowly as the new member is accepted.

If your dogs get on immediately, then they can sleep in close proximity to each other from the very start. If they seem reluctant, however, they must be kept separated; good friendships blossom over time, so don't despair. The same applies with other household pets: cats, rabbits or whatever. If they are getting along happily, then leave them together; if there is friction, separate them. Always err on the side of caution.

THE DOORWAY TO A NEW UNDERSTANDING: REUNITING

The first of the four elements of my method that you will need to tackle is reuniting after a separation. Its importance can't be overstated: it is the cornerstone of the method, the key piece of communication between dog

and owner. Yet this first hurdle is also the one that trips up many owners. In fact, in the years since I first evolved my method, no other element has been the subject of quite so many questions. This is the stage where most owners really have to overcome their human instincts and remember that they're dealing with another species. It is vital, then, that you take time to grasp this element properly. The aim of this section is to guide you and your dog through the process in simple, step-by-step detail.

I have already stressed the importance of mental preparation and of learning to think of the dog in a different way. Going into this process, you must see yourself as a member of a pack that, for the moment at least, your dog believes it is responsible for. The dog is programmed to live in a society where leadership is constantly under review. So, when the pack has been separated and is about to reunite, the dog will now need to know one thing: who is the boss now? This is your first opportunity to seize the reins of power.

I often find that owners get confused by what precisely constitutes a separation. Clearly, if your dog remains at home while a member of your family leaves the house to go to work or school for the day, or heads off to the supermarket for a couple of hours, separation has occurred. But what about when someone pops out of the living room into the kitchen, or dashes upstairs to the bathroom?

So as to clarify what I mean in my method, a separation occurs when one member of the household leaves the dog and, in so doing, erects a physical barrier between them. At this point it has become impossible for the two to communicate or connect directly. So it is not a separation when someone moves from one room to another within a house while leaving the doors open. The dog still has access to that person and can follow. If the door is closed, however, it cannot. It follows then that the first separation will occur when someone within the house leaves the dog and closes a door behind them. It is when you return to the dog's space, when you step back through that door, that you must begin to put the first principles of the method into practice.

The aim of my method is to establish a home environment into which the dog fits as naturally as every human member. My goal is to lead a dog to a situation where it is so attuned to the structure of this environment that it sees nothing unusual at all in the members of the household coming and going. The dog should accept that everyone gets on with their lives without the need to acknowledge it. It should understand that, at times, its owners are busy with other matters. There is nothing negligent or uncaring in this: in fact, quite the opposite is true. By interacting with your dog when you are ready and able to do so, you are giving your pet quality time. You will be able to shower your dog with all the love and affection it wants – the difference is that you will always be doing it on your terms.

Given all this, it therefore makes sense for the training to take place in as natural an environment as possible. Ideally, you should base the training around your normal routine. Life should go on as normally as possible, depending on the demands of your dog at particular times. Apart from anything else, this should make you and your family more relaxed about the whole process.

Stage One: the First Separation

Try to let this happen as naturally as possible – you want your dog to fit into the normal routine of the household after all. Engineered situations aren't my preferred way of working; the less artificial these first separations are the better for everyone.

Within the first few hours of the day, the moment of separation is going to come inevitably. Someone in the household is going to go to the bathroom or is going to step outside into the garden. At the same time, I understand that owners are often anxious to put the method into practice, particularly if they have made time to do this. In this case, I would suggest that, when a new dog arrives in your home, you delay the first separation until the dog has stopped its 'recce' of its new environment and has settled down. Once that has happened, you can leave the dog and move into another room, shutting the door behind you. This should be done without any ceremony. There is no need to announce it by saying 'I'm just popping out': it should not be made into an issue. By the same token, when you return to the room, you should do so quietly. Remember, the idea you want to communicate to the dog is that, as a leader of the pack, you are free to come and go as you please.

Stage Two: the Repertoire

One of two things will happen when the dog sees you have returned. It may ignore you completely; far more likely, it will go into some form of routine, a repertoire that you should recognise for what it is, the dog's attempt to establish its place in the scheme of things. It is imperative that you do not acknowledge or interact with the dog in any way, shape or form.

The following moments represent the first test of both you and your dog's determination to succeed. As I have explained, my method evolved as an alternative to the traditional forceful training regimes. Of course, you could at this point use physical force to let the dog know who is boss, however, I believe we are capable of using intellect and human resourcefulness to outmanoeuvre a dog. We do not need to be bullies or brutes to gain the dog's co-operation. Remember: 'A man convinced against his will, is of the same opinion still.'

I have seen dogs go through all sorts of repertoires in their attempt to prevail in this situation. They will leap and bound around the room, jumping on furniture, they will bark and wail and drag their favourite toys into the middle of the floor. Whatever particular act the dog treats you to, it must be ignored. By making eye contact, touching or even simply shouting 'Stop it' you are conceding defeat and acknowledging your dog's primacy. You will have confirmed the dog's belief that it is the leader.

After a while, the dog's repertoire will draw to an end. The intensity of its activity will slowly fade away. Eventually, it will either wander off or lie down on the floor, as if to signal its concession of defeat. The length of time this will take is utterly unpredictable. This can be a considerable test of your determination. Dogs are amazingly resilient and determined creatures. I have seen dogs continue with this routine for anything from a few seconds to, in the case of one particularly difficult dog, three-and-a-half hours. The average time, however, is just ten minutes. The good news, too, is that the first time is by far the worst. Once the principle has been established, it will become easier and easier to re-establish leadership. It is this first occasion that places the greatest demand on an owner.

It is an area that many owners have difficulty with, for all manner of reasons. The most common mistake people make is to assume the repertoire is over prematurely. Often, dogs go through a ten-minute routine then stop before starting again for another five minutes. Owners often mistake the break they are taking for the end of the routine.

A key signal here is the dog's body language. If your dog lies down on its side, as it would when falling asleep, it has finished its routine. But if it simply drops back onto its hind legs, Sphinx-like, with its ears pricked, its language is plain: the dog hasn't finished and is ready to spring back into action at any moment.

Many owners don't succeed in this area at first, but it should not be viewed as failure. I actually believe it should be treated as a positive event, because what must now happen is that the whole process must begin again. If you fall for this 'sucker punch', you should not beat yourself up about it. You should see it as a fresh opportunity to communicate the message to your dog and go back to the beginning of the reuniting routine. And this time your dog will get that message more quickly.

Stage Three: the Five-Minute Rule

You must now wait five minutes. Let me state here and now that I am not a major shareholder in a stopwatch manufacturing company – I do not want to be responsible for creating a world of clock-watching dog owners. Five minutes is the minimum recommended period of time: it can be as long as you like. As the method becomes ingrained in both you and your dog, it will be dramatically reduced.

The crucial point is that, during these initial stages in particular, your dog must be given time to absorb the powerful new information with which it is being provided. If it remains calm and relaxed for this period of time, you can capitalise immediately. An important breakthrough has been made. The dog has understood there has been a fundamental change in the power structure. It is vital that you now strike while the iron is hot and move on to the next stage, introducing the first basic control, 'the come'.

DEVELOPING 'THE COME'

At least five minutes after your dog has finished its repertoire, making sure you have not separated in the meantime, you should invite your dog to come to you. Once again, you should not set yourself up for failure here. In the early stages of my method, you should remember to have a food reward available whenever you are around your dog.

If necessary, you can squat or kneel at this stage. It is important that eye contact is made and your dog is called by its name. If it is a new dog, it

may not know its name yet, but the word association will quickly be made if it is repeated. The invitation you make should be warm rather than authoritarian. It should be the voice of someone inviting over a friend rather than the bark of a barrack-square sergeant major. If your dog is reluctant at first, stretch out to it, extending your arm with the food reward visible.

It is vitally important to ensure at this early stage that the food reward is presented on your terms. The sight and smell of food may well bring a dog scurrying over automatically. Dogs are opportunist eaters, remember, so premature approaches like this must be ignored. If your dog persists in trying to get at the food, remove the tidbit from sight or, if necessary, move away from the situation and begin again a few minutes later when the dog has become calm once more.

Dogs must learn from the outset that the food is not automatically theirs to enjoy. I call it a reward for good reason: they must earn it. Another key thing to watch out for here is that it is important that your dog accepts the food calmly. If the dog comes over, it should be rewarded with the food, given warm but quiet praise, and stroked or ruffled on its head, shoulders and neck. This neck area is hugely symbolic as it represents the dog's most vulnerable spot, something a leader would naturally recognise in the wild.

If your dog comes over and jumps up, or rushes at you, you must get up and walk away. You must react in the same way if your dog gets overexcited and flops over onto its back, begging to be tickled. Many owners find this difficult, but your dog must learn the consequences of its actions at this early stage. It must accept your status as the leader – and one of the leader's privileges is deciding how, when and where affection is given out. If your dog doesn't respond to the come at all, you must also walk away. In all these cases, your dog should be left alone for an hour or so before the routine is begun all over again.

This approach may seem harsh, but it is far better to turn round and restart the journey now than take this wrong turn and continue down a road that will lead to major problems later on. If you long to fuss over your dog, all you have to do is get up from where you are, walk across the room and call your dog to you. If it complies with this, you can make all the fuss of the dog you like!

Your goal is that, by the end of the first separation, your dog should have learned to relax completely, come to you on request and accept a food reward without leaping in your face. Of course, it is not always going to happen at the first attempt.

How to Know When Your Dog Has Accepted You As Leader

Dogs will, of course, manifest their personalities in different ways. Some will signal their relaxed state in obvious ways, by lying down or playing with a toy, chewing on a bone or quietly grooming themselves. But you can also look out for subtler signals.

The Eyes Have It: A key technique for spotting that your dog has relaxed lies in its eyes. If your dog is staring wide-eyed, then it is still in an anxious state: it has not accepted what is going on. If, on the other hand, the eyes are soft, then it is relaxed and ready to be called over.

A Bridge of Sighs: An important indicator of a dog's level of anxiety is its breathing rate. If it is breathing heavily and rapidly, it is still stressed, so wait until the breathing rate has steadied. The telltale sign that it has relaxed is when it releases a long, deep, peaceful sigh. In humans, a sigh is an ambiguous signal: it can mean frustration, boredom or defiance. In this situation with dogs, however, I always interpret it as a release of stress. A weight has been lifted off your dog's shoulders, and it is relieved to see it gone.

This relief can, in some cases, manifest itself in the most graphic way. I have seen marked changes in the toiletry habits of some dogs. They urinate and defecate in much larger quantities. In the case of the urine, it is easy to see why this is happening: while the dog retained its status as leader, it instinctively retained large quantities of its urine for territorial marking purposes. Freed from the responsibility of leadership, it empties its bladder in full. I must confess I was taken aback when I first encountered this. It also made me realise how 'bottled up' dogs are when they reluctantly cling to the reins of power within their pack.

Stretching Out: Some dogs will go through a routine of stretching, much like a human might do getting out of bed in the morning. They will arch their backs and splay their legs out in front of them, as in the picture below. This is a positive sign. It means the dog is relaxing.

Lip Reading: As they weigh up the situation, some dogs will begin licking their lips a lot. This is a positive rather than a negative sign. We humans do this when we are apprehensive or deep in thought; in the dog's case it is a signal that it, too, is thinking, probably wondering: 'What's going on here?' The important thing is to let your dog arrive at its decision. It will get there in its own good time.

There are, then, many indicators. But, if you are still unsure whether your dog has relaxed, you can carry out a simple test by moving from where you are sitting to another position. If your dog is relaxed, it will not react to this. If it makes a move, more time – and more patience – is required.

FREQUENTLY ASKED QUESTIONS

What's Wrong with My Dog Being Leader?

The simplest way to answer this much-asked question is with another question: would you hand over the responsibility for running your household to a one-year-old child? I often say that we keep dogs as puppies for life. By this I mean they never learn to fend for themselves in any meaningful way. They are, in effect, permanent one-year-olds, yet many, many owners inadvertently tell these immature animals that they expect them to perform the role of leader of the entire household.

This situation is clearly disastrous for all sorts of reasons. The dog has no way of understanding our society or language and, by elevating it to a job it is utterly unequipped to deal with, the owner places it in an awful position. It goes out into a world filled with a thousand threats, unable to cope with any of them. The result of this is that the dog feels a failure. And from there a vicious circle begins: as it fails to lead effectively, it gets more stressed and its behavioural problems are going to begin.

People often say to me that their dog has a natural air of leadership and may be frustrated or unfulfilled by being 'demoted'. Of course, some dogs do have a more dominant air than others; if these dogs are members of an extended pack, they will tend to head the subordinate pecking order within that pack. But even these types of dogs are happiest in an environment they understand, running free in open spaces, eating, sleeping and playing within a safe and secure pack environment.

What If My Dog Misbehaves Because it is Being Ignored?

Some hyperactive and aggressive dogs can work themselves up into a terrible state when they are given the cold shoulder in the way I advocate. They are used to demanding and getting attention. When this is denied them, they react according to their natures by selecting one of the three 'F's – flight, freeze or, in the worst-case scenario, fight. They can bark loudly, jump up into your face, or even bite. Introducing my communication method to such dogs requires a measure of planning and perseverance, but the results will be just the same.

If you have a dog with a strong personality like this, you should think about putting a collar on them before beginning. You should also prepare a room or an area of the garden where the dog can be safely excluded if necessary. In this respect, planning the geography of the training area is a classic example of being properly prepared before beginning. I advocate using a room for training and another room as an exclusion zone. If you think there is the remotest chance of your dog becoming hyperactive and 'trashing' the room, then you must clear out the room before starting, so as not to set yourself up for failure.

When the first reunion occurs after separation, if your dog reacts in an unacceptable way, you should take it by the collar and lead it away from the room to its exclusion zone. This is a crucial moment in the struggle for leadership of the pack, so it is vital that you demonstrate all the qualities of leadership at this point. You must not shout, you must not get upset and you must not speak to or acknowledge your dog in any way. Your pulse rate must remain low, and you must act firmly and decisively.

When you put your dog into a room or out into the garden, you must shut the door behind it. Eventually the dog will calm down and be quiet. Ten seconds after it has fallen silent, you should open the door and let your dog back into the main room. If the dog repeats the behaviour of earlier, you must immediately lead it back into the exclusion zone, shut the door and wait for it to become quiet again. This time you should wait a longer period, say thirty seconds. If your dog is still quiet after this time, let it back into the room. If the bad behaviour starts again, repeat the process. Each time this is repeated, your dog should take a step in the right direction. The intensity of its barking or bounding should diminish, and the length of time it remains quiet while waiting to be released from the exclusion zone should increase.

In really extreme cases, for instance if your dog bites, I suggest you attach a lead to its collar. The dog should be led out from the main room to the exclusion zone at a safe length. If a dog is so agitated it is difficult to even lead it out of the room, I ask owners to reverse the process and to leave the room themselves. You must then wait until ten seconds or so after the dog has quietened down before going into the room. The instant the bad behaviour is resumed, you must remove yourself again, returning this time thirty seconds after the dog quietens down. As before, this process must be repeated until the dog has conceded defeat and relaxed.

It can be very hard work. I have worked with owners who have had to go through this routine seven or eight times, but I cannot overemphasise how important it is to remain determined. The lessons your dog is learning at this point are life-changing. By the end of the process it should have redefined its status within the domestic pack and, at the same time, it should have understood the consequences of misbehaving. We are attempting to stage a peaceful revolution here. By overcoming this particular hurdle, you will have made the crucial first move and will have stormed the barricades – by stealth.

What About Nervous Rescue Dogs?

Too many people forget that dogs are living, breathing and – most of all – feeling creatures. Like us, they develop according to their own abilities, and we must be prepared to accommodate that into our lives. We are not programming a video recorder here, we are asking creatures to make adjustments to their ways of thinking. So it follows that getting them to understand the powerful signals within my method is something that is going to take more time in some cases than in others. And in the case of some rescue dogs, this can take a significant amount of time.

To my mind there are no such things as 'problem dogs', but there are dogs with problems. Rescue dogs have come to sanctuaries or rescue centres because they have been mistreated by humans in some respect. In some cases, of course, they have simply been abandoned. In the more extreme cases – and there are more of them than I care to think about – their experience of life with humans has been wretched. A dog may have been mistreated for years before it is rescued, and the damage done during this period is not going to be undone overnight. For this reason, you should think of these dogs as animals with learning disabilities – sometimes severe ones. You must realise that, while the dog will learn, it is going to do so at a slower rate. And it is going to need that extra bit of love, patience and understanding to get there.

How Can I Include Young Children in the Method?

Young children are clearly not going to be able to grasp the principles of my method instantly. In time, as the rest of the family masters the process they will see how things work and be more receptive to copying what their parents, brothers and sisters are doing. It is going to be a gradual process.

Having stated this, however, the smallest members of the household can make a contribution to correcting a dog's mindset. Children are never alone in the house so, invariably, the major reunions of the day will involve the children arriving home with you. They may be returning home from the shops or school, and this is where you can dispense a double dose of medicine. By steering your children away from the dog when they first enter the house, you can engineer the situation so that the children are also withholding the acknowledgement and homage that the dog expects. If, for instance, a child is placed in its high chair and distracted by a toy, a drink or some food, it will be oblivious to the dog's attention-seeking repertoire.

If, once the five-minute rule has been applied, the child is then involved in calling and rewarding the dog, an important statement will have been made about the status of this member of the family within the domestic pack. Obviously, this is not a situation that is going to be possible at all times, but it will do no harm to establish the idea in the dog's mind.

When Should I Next Separate from My Dog?

Separation is an intrinsic part of the life you and your dog are going to lead together. On the first day, however, I ask owners to minimise the amount of times that they separate from their dogs. After the first successful come, for instance, you can continue calling your dog to you while you remain together. You can also build up so that you begin playing with the dog too. Your desire to bond with the dog – especially if it is a new arrival in the home – will be considerable and understandable. The only thing I ask is that you are cautious with the amount of affection you give your dog during this very early stage. It is all too easy to drown a dog with too much affection, making it hyperactive, needy and potentially problematic further down the line.

It is also not necessary for you to interact with your dog after each and every separation. By simply ignoring the dog and going on with your daily routine, you are still relaying the central message that you are in charge of its movements. The fact that the dog is not invited to join you will further underline the message that it is you who dispenses affection and social activity within the pack.

It is also likely that other members of the household will be entering the house, and they will hopefully underline this message. Again, this is where preparation is so vital. With the dog now established in its den, all newcomers to that den must now assert themselves as a senior member of the pack immediately. They must start as they mean to go on. This, I realise, is going to be particularly hard when a member of the family comes home to meet a new dog for the first time. Hard as it may be for them to ignore the bouncing ball of fun that has just arrived in their home, they must do so until it quietens down. Like everyone else in the house, once they have applied the five-minute rule, they are free to welcome the dog to the house with affection and praise.

When Can I Stop Ignoring My Dog Each Time We Reunite?

The answer to this commonly asked question is: never. My method is not a training scheme that is dropped when it has achieved its desired effect: it is a lifestyle. If you begin acknowledging your dog when you reunite, the dog will soon claim leadership. This must not happen.

At first, many owners are daunted and discouraged by this prospect. What they soon realise, however, is that three things will happen within a short period of time. Firstly, the routine they have begun to practise will become second nature. They will automatically ignore the dog on first being reunited with them. Secondly, and more importantly, the dog's repertoire of attention-seeking behaviour will fade away. As a result of this – finally – they are able to reduce the amount of time they have to wait before calling the dog to them. Gradually, the five minutes is reduced to mere seconds.

I understand why it is difficult for owners to see this in the difficult early days. But I promise that, fairly quickly, you will be able to return to the house after a day's work and, by the time you have walked past the dog, carried on to the end of the hall and taken off your coat, your pet will have completed its ritual and will be relaxed. So well established will the routine be by now that you will then be able to immediately call the dog to come to you and reward them with all the praise and affection you like.

WALK TALL:
LEARNING THE ART OF LEADERSHIP

'The leader must know, must know that he knows, and must be
able to make it abundantly clear to those about him that he
knows.'
                                                    Clarence B. Randall

My method requires all owners to assume the leadership qualities
their domestic pack demands of them. Time and again, however, I
have seen that this is an area where many come unstuck. Many
people find it hard to impose themselves as the dominant force in the
household. There can be all sorts of reasons for this: some people are
simply shy and lacking in confidence; others are gentle souls who just
aren't used to taking the lead or expressing their personalities in such
a forceful way. Yet, in every case, I believe a little knowledge can
prove a powerful thing.

By demonstrating the five key qualities below, all owners can
quietly and efficiently take on the mantle of leader within their own
particular pack.

Walk Tall
A great deal of leadership is down to projection. Body language is a
means of communication that dogs understand all too well. They will
pick up on anyone who seems tentative or weak immediately.
Equally, they will respond immediately to someone who displays
obvious signs of authority. As we all know, first impressions are
lasting impressions, so it is vital that you present the right image
from the very first minute of the first day. Walk with an upright,
confident posture. Keep your head high, and your eye level above
that of the dog. Avoid any eye contact until you are ready to interact
with the dog.

Be Decisive

A leader's actions should be firm, final – and immediate. Your dog will test this from the start, so it is vital that you are not thrown by behaviour like gesturing or barking. You must continue to ignore the dog until you are ready to acknowledge its presence, and rebuff it immediately if it comes to you uninvited. Even allowing it to rest against your leg for a few seconds allows the dog to believe it has some authority.

Silence is Golden

We have all met owners who talk incessantly at their dogs: 'Good boy, here boy, that's my boy.' This is counter-productive, as the constant noise becomes nothing more than a background drone. Dogs respond much better to a leader who speaks only when they have got something important to say.

Speak with Authority

It is vital that your tone of voice is consistent with the body language you display. I ask owners to speak clearly, confidently and decisively. Short phrases or words are best: 'Come', 'Sit', 'Stay', all convey powerful yet simple messages. Think of the most effective leaders in our lives: none of them minces their words. Deliver praise with a smile and an extra softness to the voice, using brief phrases like: 'Good dog', 'Good, clean dog' or 'Clever dog'. My method is not so cold and mechanical that there is no room for affection either. I sometimes can't resist saying: 'I do love you'.

Believe in Yourself

Of paramount importance in my method are the two 'C's, being calm and consistent. To these two requirements, however, we need to add a third C. You must be *convincing* to the dog, and this is not going to happen unless you believe in yourself.

Many dog owners are beaten before they begin. Rather than convincing themselves that they know what they are doing, they convince themselves of the opposite. In their minds they think success is beyond them. Often, my most important job is to persuade the owner that the goal is not as impossible as it appears. Invariably these people are convinced they are simply not 'leadership material'. They are certain they are not strong enough to take charge of a situation and to have their pet believe in them. A typical example I have worked with was Anne, a single girl, in her twenties, living alone with her schnauzer, Teddy, in Kent.

Anne called me because she was having problems with him. Schnauzers have big personalities, they have a lot of attitude. Teddy was running away a lot and was pushing Anne around at home. When I met Anne, I saw that she was a small person, just over five feet tall. She was also slight in personality and was a very nervous, insecure person. I sensed that Teddy was aware of this too. It was clear almost immediately that, as long as she remained like this, Teddy was never going to relinquish the role of leader within their domestic pack. As I chatted to Anne, I explained that the onus was on her to change things. 'For the first time in your life I want you to take charge,' I told her.

There are, of course, physical reasons why some people find it difficult to impose leadership. Bigger dogs are powerful animals and owners who are small or frail can find them hard to deal with. Yet there is no reason why owners cannot behave in an authoritative way. If I am helping someone who finds themselves at a physical disadvantage with their dog I encourage them to walk away. If the dog invades their space or tries to impose itself on a situation, I tell them to leave the room and shut the door behind them. The response must be decisive and instant. If the dog sees its attempts to manipulate the situation are a total failure, it will quickly get the message.

In Anne's case, this was not necessary. She was physically capable of dealing with Teddy: it was her leadership qualities that she needed to work on. My task is often to change the way both the owner and their dog think. It is not my place to make them follow my method: I must make them want to do it. If the owner wants to change the way they communicate with their dog, then the knock-on effect will be that the dog will want to live that way too. It is one of the key areas to unite us as species: as long as there is something in it for us, we will go along with a situation.

We set about working in my normal way. After applying the five-minute rule, I asked Anne to call Teddy to her. I asked her to do it in an inviting way. At first she was tentative. So I asked her to say it again as if she really meant it. She asked Teddy to come, but this time she said it boldly, there was warmth and strength in her voice. Teddy looked at her. He sensed there was something different and came to her almost instantly. It was a promising beginning.

When I go on a call, I am putting the brakes on a downward spiral. Success breeds success and, when you get success, you become more confident. The dog realises you have that confidence which leads to more success and more confidence and so the upward spiral begins. A month down the line, Teddy and Anne were doing fantastically well. I could hear from Anne's voice that she was gaining confidence. When I spoke to her three months later, it was the changes in Anne that again struck me the most. She was speaking with so much more confidence. She was still a quiet, self-effacing woman, but at the same time she seemed more sure of herself. We ended up having a long chat, and it emerged that she had started to socialise and had made a friend of another woman who walked her dog. 'It is all to do with the belief I now have that I know what I am doing,' Anne admitted.

I must admit I became very attached to Anne and we spoke again over the following months. She worked as a sales person for a pharmaceutical company. At one point she told me she had moved on to a better job within the industry. Again she had become aware of her abilities at her work and had reaped the benefits of this self-knowledge. What I now realise is that Anne's need to communicate was as strong as her dog's. She has not become an extrovert, the personality of the year, but she's certainly become a lot more confident and more outgoing. It was wonderful to be a witness to this transformation.

FAMILY REUNIONS:
REUNITING WITH MULTIPLE PACKS

If there has been one dominant theme in the questions I have fielded since the publication of my first book, it is the issue of introducing my method to more than one dog. So many people now seem to have a number of dogs, and so many of them have asked me about this, that I feel I should devote some time to their concerns. I am not surprised at their worries. Quite naturally these owners assume that, because the dynamics of a pack of dogs are so much more complicated, the method must therefore be equally convoluted. The good news is that the principles underpinning my method remain exactly the same. The even better news is that teaching a number of dogs together is, to my mind, easier than working with a solo dog.

Essentially, you have three options available to you. Dogs can be taught either individually or as a group, or larger packs can be taught with a blend of both – as a series of groups or 'mini packs'. To decide which of these suits you best, you must be aware of the relationships your dogs have with each other. The politics of the pack is going to be an enormously useful tool and, for you to understand them, you should have an understanding of the natural society from which your dogs have come.

Pack Awareness

Each pack is unique. No matter what the mixture, whether they be dogs of the same breed or a blend of different dogs, the web of relationships they contain is different. For this reason, you must be aware of and understand the dynamics within your pack, to avoid being caught out. By underestimating the forces at work within a pack, you run the real risk of setting yourself up for failure.

Ultimately, the forces that drive a pack are no different from those that drive an individual dog: survival is the ultimate priority for both. Once more, the roots of those instincts lie within the dogs' ancient ancestors and community, the wolf pack. For millennia, the wolf has steadfastly accepted the hierarchical principles that underpin pack life. The Alpha pair command complete respect. Their primacy is beyond challenge and the rest of the pack feel safe in the knowledge that the pack is their best option for survival.

The remainder of the pack has its own ranking system, ranging from second-in-command Beta males and females, to yearlings and pups. Each has a clear grasp of its job description, whether it be joining the Alphas on the hunt or remaining in the den on guard duty. The complex variations need not exercise us too much: the key point to understand here is that the lower-ranking wolves are all perfectly happy in the subordinate roles they occupy beneath their leaders. As long as the pack survives the tests of everyday life, the wolves are content with the ranking they have at this lower level. It is akin to a successful corporation run by a charismatic, intelligent and hugely resourceful chief executive: Richard Branson is the obvious example here in the UK. The corporation's staff believes in this leader totally. Their lives depend on the company's success and they know he's their best chance of delivering it to them. They believe in the power structure that has been assembled below him because it works.

But a company does not become successful by resting on its laurels. And it will not survive, let alone thrive, if it takes anything for granted. Therefore, the leader is constantly being observed by his staff, his mettle is perpetually being tested. The leader knows this, and uses the fact that he is constantly being judged to his advantage. He knows that, as long as he continues to exude an air of confidence, that confidence will seep through the ranks. There will, of course, be rivalries and allegiances within the ranks, just as there are in any company: not everyone is going to get along. And if the leader is lost, those rivals will battle it out to succeed him. But, unless the company's existence is threatened, everyone is more than happy to abide by the pecking order. The status quo will be maintained. It suits everyone.

This is how I ask owners to think of their domestic pack. Dogs are naturally submissive creatures – they will do anything for a quiet life. It is why they allow humans to bully them so easily, but is also why they are so willing to be led by others. A pack is at its happiest when there is a sense of natural order, a harmony among the dogs. They will test the leader particularly at the four occasions when the pack's survival is on the line: when reuniting after separation, at feeding time, at times of danger and during the hunt. Provided they are confident in the abilities of their leader to deal with these situations, they will fall into line behind them.

It is important to realise, however, that each pack will have its own dynamic. Dogs are, as I have emphasised before, living, feeling creatures. So, inevitably, there will be alliances and rivalries, some dogs who are close friends and others who simply don't get on. This is easy to detect: dogs that dislike each other will turn their backs on each other or avoid eye contact. They will keep a distance between themselves, and take positions at different ends of the room – their body language is obvious. There will also be occasions when these tensions are more likely to surface. These are usually connected with times of uncertainty such as when new dogs arrive or old dogs leave, or when members of the pack are in season.

Some other alliances will be equally easy to read. Blood ties will obviously be tight, but that does not mean there cannot be sibling rivalries too. Equally, there will be some dogs that are more dominant than others. It is something I have seen in all my packs. In my first book, I talked about Donna, the dog we called 'The Duchess'. She expected everyone, human and canine, to defer to her: she was a rare, natural Alpha. This is often a matter of sheer personality. The crucial thing to realise here is that all these things are within a dog's nature and we cannot do anything about them. The one exception to this is, just because we cannot fight nature, does not mean that we should let dogs fight: violence and aggression between pack members must never be allowed. In general, the pack's overriding instinct is to preserve the status quo, to keep things as they are. They know they are better off together, that there is strength in numbers and in the concept of community. These are powerful forces that can be used to your advantage.

✻   ✻   ✻

My own dogs have offered me some of the most telling insights into the diverse forces that bind together – and sometimes tear apart – a pack. This was never more the case than in the wake of the dramatic events following the deaths of Sasha and Barmie. What I witnessed, of course, was a fight for a leadership role that I had myself relinquished. By looking at the dynamics that had for years underpinned the pack, I can see that the events that occurred were, sadly, all too predictable.

Like all packs, my dogs had their own, unique history. Its roots stretched back more than six years, to a period when I had just lost my previous generation of dogs. At that time, Sasha and Barmie were my only dogs, and they were inseparable. The pack began to expand when Sasha gave birth to Sadie. She was the only one of a litter of shepherds that I kept. By this time I had decided to move back into the breeding and showing world. It was with this in mind that I took in Molly, a fine springer spaniel.

Throughout this period there was no doubt which dog held primacy within the pack: it was Sasha. She was not only the first dog to have joined the household but, far more importantly, she was also the first to breed. In the wild, as we know, only the Alpha is permitted to breed. Since the arrival of Sadie, Sasha's sense of superiority had deepened. Just how seriously she took this role became clear when Molly fell pregnant. The fact that Molly was breeding at all put Sasha's defences up immediately. It cannot have made much sense, given what her instincts told her about non-Alphas not being able to breed.

Yet, afterwards, Sasha was hugely protective of the two puppies I kept, Jake and Jen. I recall one occasion when Molly growled at her puppies for some reason. Sasha stepped in immediately. Her message was clear: 'I am in charge here and you do not have the right to treat them like this.' This pattern continued when other members bred. The first to do this was Jen, who produced Reef and Opal. Then, soon after I incorporated another springer, Ceri, into the pack she gave birth to her puppies Todd and Gabby.

When Sasha died, it was only natural that there should be a challenge for the leadership of the canine wing of my pack. If I had not proven myself such an inadequate leader at the crucial first reunion after saying goodbye to Sasha, this process would have been far less dramatic. The fact remains that I did fail in my leadership that day – and it was entirely predictable how the rivalries panned out.

In terms of seniority, Sasha's daughter, Sadie, was the longest-serving member of the pack. She'd always been Sasha's natural second-in-command too. It was inevitable that she would have some say in matters. A far stronger factor, however, was the rivalry between the two springer mothers, Ceri and Molly. At first I was stunned at Molly's attack on Ceri. She had always been what I call a 'Cinderella' dog: good-natured, easy-going and non-confrontational. I was at a loss to understand why she had turned into an aggressive and ambitious Ugly Sister.

It was not long before I saw the mechanics of the situation, however. In many ways, a pack responds to the loss of its leader in the same way as a political party. When a politician stands down, there is always an unsightly dash to claim the crown. The pecking order that existed previously counts for nothing. The reality was that my pack had become leaderless. Molly had more invested in the pack than any other member – after all it contained two of her children and two of her grandchildren too. She knew that a new leader had to be installed immediately. The queen was dead, and a new queen had to be crowned that instant. And in this situation, all her normal reticence and good nature had no place. Quite simply, Molly had no choice but to make a bid for the leadership of the pack.

Viewed from this perspective, I can see why these two matriarchal figures came to exchange the first physical blows of the leadership campaign. Clearly, very few owners will be faced with circumstances like this: I certainly hope they won't! But, as they begin to implement my method, all owners should try to pinpoint the structure of their pack. It will prove priceless in the days and weeks ahead.

Teaching a Pack As Individuals

Every owner's circumstances are, of course, going to be different. It simply may not be possible for you to cope with the process of working two or more dogs at the same time. Equally, there may be particular tensions within the pack that prevent pack work. Clearly, for some owners, the best option is going to be working with the dogs individually. The key thing here is that, by the end of the process, the pack has been brought together. This way you will benefit from all the positive interactive forces within the pack.

You should begin the process by isolating one dog at a time from the pack and going through the initial technique of reuniting after a separation. If one dog within the pack is particularly problematic, disruptive, or simply more high-spirited than the rest, I would recommend leaving this one until last. Certainly in the case of rescue dogs, which are generally highly nervous animals, this is by far the most desirable way of beginning. My reasoning here is simple and based on personal experience. If a difficult dog rejoins the pack to discover its peers in a relaxed and cooperative mood, it becomes far more receptive to the idea of joining this responsive state. The influence it sees you wielding over its pack colleagues is hugely powerful. By the same token, the dominant dog should be worked first if possible. The knowledge that this dog has accepted you as leader will be a hugely powerful weapon with the rest of the pack.

When you are ready to begin reuniting work, your first dog should be disregarded in the way I have already described. Again, it is important to stress that this process cannot be rushed. Dogs will surrender themselves according to their own timetable, so if you are going to attempt to work with a number of dogs in this way, you must put aside a sizable amount of time to put this into practice.

The first dog should go through its repertoire and relax entirely. Once this has been achieved, the next member of the pack should be brought into the room. Almost certainly at this point, dog number one will revert to its repertoire again. This is perfectly natural – after all, the two dogs are reuniting after a separation as well. The likelihood is, however, that the repertoire will last for a shorter period of time. The key thing to observe here is that both dogs reach the point of relaxation before you move on. Once the dogs have reached this point, the next dog must be brought in. This time all three must calm down before moving on.

This process should continue until the last dog has rejoined the pack. As I have said, I recommend that the most disruptive dog within the pack should be left until last. Hopefully this dog will enter a room in which it finds that its peers are displaying homage to a powerful new leader. It will almost inevitably attempt to subvert this process. But, by remaining calm and displaying convincing leadership, you should eventually see the whole pack reaching a relaxed state. It is now that the five-minute rule should be applied. Again, it is worth stating that this is only a minimum period: reaching this point may well be a long, hard struggle. Provided you do not separate from your pack, you may well want to take a longer break.

The Come

When you are ready to carry on, you must now build on the level of leadership you have already achieved. And the way to do this is by establishing that you have the power to choose which dog you interact with from now on. At this point, call one of the dogs to you: it doesn't matter which one it is. It is important that you only look at and acknowledge the dog you have called and ignore the others. Any dog that runs up or attempts to jump up must be steered away firmly but fairly. In contrast, the dog that has been called to come should be rewarded generously when it does so.

This process should then be repeated with other members of the pack. As each of them learns to come to you as requested, it should be rewarded in the same way. Each time one of the dogs behaves inappropriately by coming when it has not been called, it should be ignored and, if necessary, gently rebuffed by you, the leader. This is a potent time. The pack as a whole is seeing a radical new form of communication. A seismic shift in the hierarchy of the extended pack has occurred. Things will never be the same again.

If you own a particularly nervous dog, I would recommend that you leave it alone. Such dogs tend to remain disconnected, almost aloof from the rest of the pack during this process. There is nothing wrong with allowing it to stay on the fringe of things. As I have explained, it is not necessary for you to interact with a dog each time you reunite. Besides, simply observing the rest of the pack in action will act as a powerful stimulus for it.

The nervous dog will signal its readiness to interact soon enough. It is important to remember, of course, that you should not let the dog make the first move, no matter how much you are looking forward to that first affectionate moment. There can be no predicting at what time this will happen and you certainly shouldn't expect it to happen in an instant. Like all good things, however, it is worth waiting for.

Teaching Dogs As a Pack

I often say it is easier to train two dogs than one. By this I mean that there are strong forces at work within a pack of two or more dogs that can be channelled by an intelligent owner. Essentially, pack teaching involves applying en masse the individual method outlined above. The process begins with all members of the pack present. When all the dogs have exhausted their repertoire and have relaxed, individuals should then be asked to come in turn. For fairly obvious reasons, this is only going to be practical with small packs of two to four dogs. The potent peer pressure applied by their fellow dogs, along with the animal's deep-seated need to belong to a pack, are invaluable tools.

I have come across no better an illustration of this power of the pack than the case of Dish and Spoon, a pair of Jack Russell terriers who had grown from being inseparable friends to lethal rivals. Their owners, George and Estelle, had taken them into their home, an old rectory near Louth in Lincolnshire, as puppies from the same litter. As puppies, they had played incessantly – exactly as they should – using the experience of tugging and pulling and wrestling with each other as a means of developing a whole range of skills. Three years on, however, the pair's habit of wrestling with each other had taken on a much more sinister and upsetting form. They would regularly egg each other on. In the fights that ensued, they had suffered bites and punctures to ears, lips and legs.

George and Estelle were devoted to their dogs and had done all they could to help Dish and Spoon. A vet had recommended that the more aggressive of the pair, Spoon, be castrated. I may not win very many friends in the veterinary world for saying this, but I am against castration as a means of calming aggressive behaviour in dogs. The procedure obviously has its place in the dog world – in medically necessary cases and where dogs need to be stopped from reproducing. My objections tie in with my general overview of dog behaviour. Castration does nothing to relieve the dog of its delusions of power. All it does is lower its testosterone level and create an even more wounded animal. The less it feels able to do the job of leader, the more panic-stricken and the more aggressive it becomes.

As it turned out, events with Dish and Spoon bore out my case. The castration did little to calm Spoon down. In fact he became more aggressive. The vet then suggested that Dish be castrated. The results were, to my mind, inevitable. One day, George and Estelle were in the garden with the two dogs when Spoon suddenly flew at Dish and launched the most ferocious attack either of them had ever seen. The spectacle of your own two dogs trying to rip each other to pieces is a shattering thing for a dog lover to behold. The dogs were left in a dreadful state afterwards. Dish had a gaping hole in his chest. Spoon had puncture wounds on his face and legs. It was at this point that George and Estelle called me in.

As I listened to their story, I sensed how heartbreaking it had been for George and Estelle to see such great sibling ties broken. I explained to them that, in applying my method, they could use those ties to rekindle and revive the brothers' old relationship.

It was clear to me that the root of Dish and Spoon's problem lay in their competing wish to lead the pack. This was obvious from the times when George and Estelle told me trouble flared up most easily. Predictably, these were when people came to the door or walked past the gate outside, when there was an aircraft passing overhead or, sometimes, when Estelle was preparing food. I knew that the powerful bond that once connected these dogs had to be used to bring them together once more.

As I began, the key thing was to let each dog see the other undergoing the process. The two dogs were separated by a gate between the kitchen and the sitting room so that, while I was working with Dish, Spoon could see clearly what was happening and vice versa. I went through the usual five-minute rule routine. I was encouraged early on by the fact that, rather than focusing on the other dog, the dog I was working with gave its full attention. Also, I noticed a distinct lessening of the growling coming from the non-participating dog as it watched the other dog respond to the signals I was giving it. Eventually, encouraged by the other's behaviour, it too calmed down. I then worked on the come, with both dogs still isolated but within view of each other.

After a while, I suggested we took the two dogs for a walk on leads in the garden. George and I took them out, being careful to keep them in opposite parts of the garden. They eyed each other up for a while. Slowly, however, both relaxed, allowing us to bring them closer and closer together. It was not long before they were wagging their tails and looking at each other. 'It was as if they were meeting each other for the first time,' George said.

I knew there was still a long way to go, and suggested we now walk them alongside each other. Once again, I was going to use the natural power of the pack here. It was not long before Spoon gave a low grumble at Dish. I immediately led him away from the garden into a room in the house. I now wanted to use the dogs' natural need for companionship and the safety of numbers as a lever. As Spoon was removed, his body language told its own story. It was slumped, much like a sulking teenager who has just been sent to his room. Spoon was clearly hugely disappointed at being separated like this. Deep down, he had a desperate desire to be with his sibling. I released him from his room after fifteen minutes. He behaved slightly better but growled again after a while. Once more, he was banished to the room. Once more we saw the sulky stoop.

George and Estelle grasped what was going on. They could see that, with each separation, Spoon's attitude to Dish was changing. He was realising significant changes were afoot. By the end of my visit there, George and

Estelle felt very positive and assured me they would build on this. Over the following weeks, they worked on these early break-throughs, and soon Dish and Spoon were able to go out for short walks together in the garden. At this point, however, they were both still on the lead.

I suggested to George and Estelle that the first occasion they let the two dogs off the leash together should take place on neutral ground. Six weeks later, I got a phone call from them asking if I'd be willing to join them when they released the two dogs in a friend's garden. Of course, I was pleased to be there.

On the big day, George took one dog while I took the other. Slowly we lowered the leads to the floor and let them go. To our delight, the two dogs just carried on investigating the garden, heading in different directions. I remember George gave my hand a squeeze, but I quickly cautioned him against getting too optimistic.

In the weeks that followed, Dish and Spoon could be left off the lead without any confrontations. Things have improved steadily from there. The old friendship has been restored, yet common sense has had to prevail too. As a sensible precaution, George and Estelle now always separate them whenever they get too exuberant. And they always make sure the pair are separated when they are left on their own together at home. These small sacrifices have been more than worthwhile, however. To see the siblings together and happy again after all they have been through is a joy.

Group Therapy

The third option for introducing my method applies in larger packs, where, for purely practical reasons, owners may find it easier to work with smaller, more manageable groups of dogs. This approach may also suit some owners who have a mixture of puppies and adult dogs. Given the high energy levels of the puppies, it may be easier to work with the younger dogs separately from the older dogs.

Whatever the reason for the decision, the method should be the same. Take each group and teach them together, in the way outlined above.

When you have achieved success with both groups separately, you can then move towards gradually integrating the whole pack. This is not something that should happen in one move. If you feel happy and in control, move on – if not, don't. You should integrate the various factions and family groupings slowly, again using the pack dynamics to work in your favour.

It was this approach that I chose when it came to reintroducing my method to my dogs in the wake of Sasha's and Barmie's deaths. I have to admit that, in the time since I began developing and practising my method, this was the hardest thing I have had to do. It felt like I had hit a wall. I really didn't know how I was going to go on. As I pulled myself together and faced up to the responsibility, however, a few things became crystal clear. Given the divisions that had opened up within the group, I knew it would be impossible to work with them as a whole group. At the same time, I knew that I could use the allegiances that existed to weld different elements of the pack together. And I sensed that Molly was the key to the equation as I attempted to put my pack back together again.

I isolated Molly so that she was on her own. I knew that what she had done was natural and instinctive and I didn't want to punish her for that. In reality, I also knew that, if I had been a more effective leader when I'd returned home that day, Molly would not have needed to transform herself in such a way. It was my fault, not hers, but at the same time she had to be shown that her behaviour was totally unacceptable. She had started the trouble, and I could not condone violence in any shape or form within our pack. In the few days it took me to prepare myself for the task, I kept my dogs in their separate groups: Sadie with Jake and Reef; Molly with her daughter and granddaughter, Jen and Opal; and Ceri with her pups. These were the most natural groupings possible and ensured a calm atmosphere returned to the home.

When the time came, I spent a morning attempting to reform the pack, slowly integrating members of these three separate groups. Firstly I got Opal and Ceri together. I worked through the basic process of reuniting after a separation. The aftereffects of the previous week were still tangible. Both were much more excitable than they had been before and took longer to settle and accept my leadership than normal. In time, however, they both relaxed in each other's company. Next, I brought Jake and Reef into the room with us. Again, their arrival caused a degree of excitement, but it was time for me to reassert myself as leader and after a few minutes I achieved this. The four dogs were happy in each other's company again.

Next I introduced poor Sadie to them. I must confess my heart had gone out to her over the previous days. She had lost her mother, after all, and I had taken her out for walks on her own, but I had been aware of not smothering her in affection. I didn't want her to misinterpret my meaning, she had to re-elect me leader too! Sadie had inherited much of her mother's intelligence and quickly cottoned on to what was going on. Again, her nature desperately wanted the pack to be pulled together again. Soon she, too, was happy in her old friends' company again.

I now had five dogs back together again. They were behaving well and had happily accepted my leadership. The next task was to bring together the dogs that had been at the epicentre of the violence: Molly and Ceri would be the last to be put together. Firstly, I tried to introduce Jen into the picture. Because I did not want to leave a dog alone, I removed Sadie and Jake from the room. I then introduced Jen to Ceri, Opal and Reef.

It was obvious that neither Jen nor Ceri had forgotten what had happened before. They immediately started circling each other. It was plain to see that, if left to their own devices, they would attack each other again. So I intervened immediately and took hold of both of them by the neck and held them on either side of me. I held them in this position for a while. They carried on looking at each other, their body language unmistakably indicating their displeasure. After a while, however, they became aware of my displeasure too. I was giving both of them the sort of scalding look my mother used to give me. Soon they had stopped making eye contact with each other and were looking up to me for guidance. I had regained their respect. They were soon relaxed in each other's company again.

By now I had spent two hours that morning. I was thinking about reuniting Molly with Sadie, but when I went to Molly's room I saw that another complication was going to be added to the picture. Telltale spots of blood lay on the floor: Molly was in season. This forced me to rethink my tactics. So I put Jen back with Molly, where she had been before. I then put Opal, Sadie, Jake, Reef and Ceri together. I now had two groupings within the pack.

All that was left now was to put together the two main protagonists, Molly and Ceri. I was really keen to push on, so that afternoon I decided to put them together in the garden. Glenn was with me in case it all flared up again. We led them both out off their leads, but as Molly came out into the garden I kept my hand on her neck, applying the slightest amount of pressure. I knew she would arch her neck the moment she saw Ceri and wanted to show her this was not what I wanted. Glenn did the same thing with Ceri. The most important thing now was that we both remained calm. The last time these two had been in each other's company, we had been hopelessly weak and they had picked up on it. This time we had to be strong. The two dogs moved around each other for a few minutes. The tension was palpable, but, thankfully, there was not a repeat of the awful violence that had occurred last time these two were together. It was the first step in the right direction.

PACK PROBLEMS

New Dogs and Existing Packs

It is, as I have already explained, imperative that you are careful about introducing new dogs – and in particular, older dogs – to existing packs. Regardless of how well attuned the existing dogs are, the arrival of a new personality can be the spark for disruption, tension and outright aggression. In the worst cases, this can have tragic consequences.

I recommend you only introduce a newcomer once you have successfully established yourself as the unchallenged leader within your existing pack. The pack-training option you use will be entirely dependent on the dynamics of the pack, of course. I would also advise that you introduce your most easy-going and friendly dogs to the newcomer first. If you have the space, work in the separate, 'neutral' area where your dogs have been getting to know each other.

Lengthy Separations

Owners of packs need to be particularly careful when the pack is split up and separated from now on. In their natural environment, dogs are simply unused to members leaving the pack for any length of time. Short separations are far less problematic, but if a dog leaves for an extended stay at the vet, or travels with you whilst the other dogs are left at home, the housebound dogs will assume the pack dynamic has changed permanently.

A good comparison might be in the workplace. Imagine someone leaving their job to join another company: their departure would cause a restructuring. What if they were then to simply show up again, expecting their old position back? This, in a nutshell, is what the pack is faced with after a lengthy separation. (In the canine case, the matter is complicated further by the fact that the returning dog arrives back imbued with strange new smells that are unfamiliar to the pack.) So the situation must be approached with great care.

What invariably happens in these situations is that the dogs that have remained at home will go into a repertoire with the dog that has been outside. To minimise the amount of aggression that occurs, I recommend that the dogs are reunited one at a time – always ensuring that none of the housebound dogs are left on their own. If a dog is left on its own in this situation it will feel it is being isolated and therefore punished for no reason. So, if there are three dogs within the pack, bring both in to meet the other when the walk is over. If there are four in the pack, bring one and then two in. If there are five, bring in one, then another, then the final two – and so on.

Training a Litter of Puppies: the Goxhill Mafia

On the face of it, the prospect of training a litter of lively puppies seems a daunting task. Controlling even one bundle of hyperactive energy appears challenging enough; attempting to impose your will on six or seven of them seems like mission impossible. I have had to deal with all manner of packs in my time, including puppies. None left an impression to compare with that of the half dozen, five-month-old, cross Border collie puppies I was called in to treat in the very early days of my work. Their case demonstrates how my method can prove remarkably easy, not to mention fun, to apply.

Puppies can bring chaos even to the most well organised homes. We're all familiar with the image of the unravelled clothing and the unfurled rolls of toilet paper tumbling down the stairs. But the very special brand of pandemonium this bunch brought to their owners, a family of six, in the village of Goxhill, Lincolnshire, almost beggared belief.

On the telephone, I had wondered whether the owners were exaggerating. They described how, at regular intervals, the puppies would sweep through the house like a tornado, leaving a trail of destruction in their wake. No sooner had I stepped through the door than I realised that the family had, in fact, been downplaying the dogs' devilish tendencies. I called them the 'Goxhill Mafia'.

The owners showed me how the kitchen bore the brunt of the storm. The puppies would help themselves to food, chomping their way through packets of biscuits and cereals; they had even bitten their way through tins. Any plates, pots and pans that stood in their way were brushed aside. Nothing, it seemed, escaped their juvenile jaws.

Over the last few months, the calamitous puppies had bitten their way through floorboards, copper piping and even an electrical cable (fortunately it had been disconnected). The family's clothing had been reduced to a pile of rags. The garden outside was a scene from a post-nuclear holocaust. The family had an elderly Yorkshire terrier; such was the mayhem the puppies were causing, he had spent three months permanently holed up upstairs. Try as the owners might, he would not venture down into the newcomers' territory.

To their eternal credit, the family was determined to find a way to integrate the puppies into their home life. They had decided to have the puppies, and felt it was their responsibility to ensure they were safe and cared for properly. Fortunately for myself and the family, the puppies' mother remained at home with her litter. Anyone tackling a pack of puppies must begin with the mother first: to her brood she exerts a powerful natural authority. If she is willing to relinquish responsibility to a new human Alpha, her innocent youngsters will swiftly follow her lead.

I worked with the mother on her own to begin with; her protective instincts would have been in overdrive if I had been working with her children at the same time. She presented no real problems and was soon relaxed. It was at this stage that I asked for the puppies to be brought in one at a time.

Separating the pack proved a real test in itself. It took three members of the family to keep the remaining five puppies on the other side of the gate in the garden, while the first of the litter came in. Predictably, the puppy went crazy when it was brought into the room with its mother. The mother displayed a little anxiety at first, but soon remembered the newly established order. It took about five minutes for the puppy to follow its mother's example. One down, five to go.

I then asked for the next puppy to be brought in. Again, the dog went into overdrive when it arrived in the room. And, as invariably happens, the first puppy resumed its leaping around too. But this situation did not last for long and, within five minutes, the second puppy had picked up on the first's example and was also nicely relaxed. I carried on this way with all seven dogs. It took roughly the same length of time to bring each of them under control. Each time a new puppy entered, the other dogs went back into their old, frantic repertoire before the lights came on and they recalled the new routine.

It was a classic example of dogs coming to a decision they knew would be of benefit to them. They identified me as a competent, convincing leader and, led by their mother's example, were happy to invest their trust in me. It was, as it should always be, no decision at all. Why be burdened with the responsibilities of leadership when someone perfectly qualified for the role was there ready and willing to take charge? In effect, I had made the Goxhill Mafia an offer they simply couldn't refuse.

It was a magic moment. Surrounded by seven placid dogs, I looked up to see a group of people with their jaws on the floor. The family's sense of disbelief deepened when a friend of one of their children arrived unexpectedly. Ordinarily, this would have been the signal for the puppies to explode into action. Instead, they looked up at me briefly then returned to their new, low-key routine when I thanked them for their help. I must admit I felt rather pleased with myself at that point.

The test then was for the family to apply the method consistently at home on their own. It took them a month of hard work – working with all the dogs in the home, not just the puppies – but they got there. After another month, even the Yorkshire terrier came downstairs. And the Goxhill Mafia, as far as I know, scared no one from then on.

FOOD POWER AND GESTURE EATING

I am a great believer in simplicity and the idea that less can often be more. So often in life, I have seen people making the mistake of over-complicating things. It is why I work hard to keep my method as straight-forward and uncomplicated as possible at all times. The simplest part of my method – and by far the easiest for people to grasp and put into practice – is what I call 'gesture eating'. It is a classic example of less sometimes being more. For all its simplicity, it may well be the most powerful signal of all.

As I have already explained, the distribution of food plays a crucial role in the life of the dog's ancient ancestors, the wolf pack. It is hardly surprising that the wolf Alpha pair are at their most dominant during the gathering and consumption of food. Their job, after all, is to preserve and protect the pack: without them, the pack would not survive. Meal times enshrine this order in the most symbolic way. By ensuring they eat first at mealtimes, the Alpha pair signal in unequivocal terms that they are the leaders. By giving their leaders first refusal at every mealtime, the rest of the pack are acknowledging that they instinctively understand this. Even if there is only enough food for two wolves, the pack will expect the Alpha pair to eat it all to ensure the survival of the pack.

Gesture eating is my way of demonstrating the owner's primacy at feeding time. It is an element I ask people to apply for a minimum of two weeks. If at all possible, I prefer every family member to participate. By acting as a team, this will allow you to communicate an immense amount of information and will establish all of you at an upper level of the household's hierarchy.

Again, the overriding priority here is to be calm and consistent, and it is essential this is repeated at all mealtimes during this period. Many people, for practical reasons I can understand, feed their dogs during the evenings only. For maximum impact, I prefer it if dogs are fed twice daily, once in the morning and again in the evening. The technique, below, is simple.

Gesture Eating, Step by Step

Step 1
Bring your dog into the kitchen or feeding area. Before preparing the dog's food, place a biscuit, cracker or any other small snack on a plate on a raised surface, such as a table or kitchen worktop. If two or more family members are present, each of you should have their own snack.

Step 2
Place your dog's bowl next to the plate. Ensure the dog is watching and prepare its meal in the normal way.

Step 3

Each family member should now eat their snack. This should be done in full view of the dog, but without anyone speaking to or acknowledging its presence. This underlines each person's status as senior members of the household hierarchy in the eyes of the dog.

Step 4

When everyone has finished eating and returned their empty plates to the table or worktop, the dog's bowl should only now be placed on the floor. Again, this must be done quickly, without any fuss. Once the dog has finished the meal, the bowl should be taken away immediately. Again the message is clear: the leader is the provider of food, and it is the leader that decides when feeding time is over.

It Is Better to Give than to Remove: 'Power Gesture Eating'

A popular argument among traditional trainers is that a powerful way of 'showing the dog its place' is taking its food away from it. I could not disagree with this more strongly. It is confrontational and potentially dangerous, particularly when the dog's previous experience is of being denied food. 'Power gesture eating' is a means for proving the opposite applies. Nothing is more certain to win a dog's devotion than being seen as a giver rather than a taker of food.

I first developed the technique to help owners who have problems with dogs that become nervous or aggressive at mealtimes. It is a problem particularly common to rescue dogs, which can snarl and snap at anyone who comes near them while they are eating. It is easy to see why they behave this way. Often these dogs arrive at sanctuaries or rescue centres having been starved close to death. When they are given food, they are desperate to hang on to it. And anyone approaching them is seen as a threat that might take that food away. Instinctively, the dog feels that it must challenge the person with the food.

One of the central aims of my approach is to instil in the dog the feeling that it always wants to be at its owner's side. There is no better way of getting this idea across. The idea is that by following the process above, the dog will form a powerful, positive association between food and its leader. It will see you as a giver. And the dog will begin to realise that wherever it finds you, so too it will find food. The process is described in the panel on the next page.

Packs: Variations on Gesture Eating

Feeding time presents a perfect opportunity for you to demonstrate leadership to the pack as a whole. It enables you to establish in the clearest language that you are responsible for the allocation of food. And it allows you to do so in full view of the gathered pack. Bearing this in mind, it is,

Power Gesture Eating, Step by Step

Step 1
Set the preparation of the meal up in the same way as normal gesture eating. Instead of putting all the dog's food in one bowl, however, divide it up into three or four smaller portions in separate bowls.

Step 2
As normal, eat a small snack in full view of the dog. Then place its first bowl of food on the floor and step back.

Step 3
As the dog completes the first bowl, place a second bowl of food down in a different area of the room. Stand by the bowl until the dog comes to it, then step away again.

Step 4
Keep repeating this for the remainder of the bowls, making sure each time the food is put down in a different location and that the dog sees who has placed it there.

however, vital that owners of multiple packs are once again aware of the subtle dynamics at work within their family of dogs. From the outset, each dog should be allocated its own spot, a clearly defined piece of territory within the dining area. This should remain the same at every feeding time from then on. Allocation of these areas should be given a great deal of thought. If there are two dogs that do not get along, it makes sense that they should not have their bowls placed adjacent to each other. You should also try to reflect the alliances within the pack, placing friendly dogs near each other.

The essential gesture-eating technique for packs remains the same as for a single dog. Another thing to bear in mind, however, is that you may easily disrupt the balance within the pack's hierarchy by feeding dogs in a specific order of preference: this could easily create tension within the pack. Given that gesture eating is going to continue for only a few weeks, it would be helpful if an extra pair of hands was available at main mealtimes. This way, the bowls could be distributed at the same moment, so as to avoid any hint of favouritism.

If, for whatever reason, you cannot feed the dogs at the same time, you should operate a strict rota system. If dog A is fed ahead of dogs B and C in that order for meal one then, when meal two arrives, dog A should be fed last, with B and C getting priority in that order. Meal three should begin with dog C being fed ahead of A then B, and so on.

FREQUENTLY ASKED QUESTIONS

My Puppy Has a Voracious Appetite. Should I Gesture Eat Every Time I Feed Him?

In a word, no. Puppies' eating habits differ wildly from those of older dogs. On average, an eight-week-old puppy needs four feeds a day. Experience has taught me that you do not necessarily need to gesture eat each time you feed a puppy; once a day is sufficient to impart the message that you are the food provider. The only thing I stress is that you must not make the mistake of leaving food down all the time. Tempting though this is with a ravenous young animal around, it undermines and negates the message you are working so hard to impart in every other area of the dog's daily life.

Should I Involve Children in Gesture Eating?

Of all the elements of my method, this is the one that lends itself most naturally to involving children. It can easily be presented to them as a game, and it can be great fun to go through this process together as a family. The only word of caution I would issue is that the gesture eating should not become a form of teasing or, even worse, humiliation. It should be done in a matter-of-fact way.

What If My Dog Likes to Snack?

One of the easiest mistakes people can make is to leave food down for a dog at all times. It sends out the worst possible signal: it allows the dog to dictate when mealtime occurs. And this simply mustn't happen. For the dog to accept you as leader, it is vital that you retain complete control of feeding time. You should decide when it begins and when it ends, and this must be adhered to rigidly.

If your dog has a habit of walking away and taking breaks during its meal, this should be discouraged by the removal of the bowl. Again, this builds on instinctive pack behaviour in the wild. If a wolf moves away from its kill, it is signalling that it is satisfied and the next member of the pack's pecking order can move in. It is not a decision that can be reversed. It is the same here: the dog must learn that, when it steps away from its food, it signals the end of the allocated feeding time. It must learn the consequences of its action. You should not worry about depriving your dog of food: it is not, I can promise you, going to starve. Dogs pick up all the signals within my method quickly, but any message relating to food is picked up that little bit quicker.

Is There a Danger of My Dog Eating Too Much?

Yes, and this is something that all owners must guard against. Once your dog has come around to your way of thinking, rewards should only be used in rare instances. During the course of the early phases of training, however, tidbits will be used on a regular basis, so it is important to ensure that the individual food rewards handed out are both modest and appropriate. I do not want to be responsible for creating a world of overweight, and therefore unhealthy, dogs. By 'modest' amounts, I mean that the food handed out should be small in size, say a half-inch piece of meat strip or a sugar-cube-sized piece of cheese. By appropriate, I mean that the food should be part of the dog's natural, healthy diet. I have come across owners who have asked me whether they can reward their dogs with chocolate or biscuits. I dread to think what the effect of this would be!

There is another reason why you must exercise caution in this area. The aim of my method is to relieve the dog of the pressures of leadership, to lift the yoke off its shoulders if you like. The advent of this new, stress-free existence can also have the effect of making your dog put on weight. The reason for this is simple: faced with the role of leading the pack day in, day out, a dog burns off calories. When this pressure leaves its life, it becomes happier, more relaxed – and potentially fatter. There are two easy ways to deal with this, of course. Your dog's diet should be monitored, and reduced if necessary, and the dog should be given as much appropriate exercise as possible. And, unlike humans, it can do this without state-of-the-art running shoes or membership of an expensive gym.

In my experience, it is rare that people encounter problems with gesture eating or the use of food rewards. Owners, in general, find the principles straightforward and easy to apply. More important still, dogs are extremely quick on the uptake in situations where food is involved. It was not merely its rarity value that made the case of Dexter the boxer so memorable, however. It was the fact that it also made me howl with laughter.

Dexter's owner, Tom, had read my first book, *The Dog Listener*, and had applied the method with great success. He and his family had been working at it for three to four weeks and were delighted with the transformation. As Tom put it to me, 'That book could have been written about Dexter.' He had every bad trait going, from jumping up to pulling on the lead, from charging at strangers to barking at the boundary fence. All of these had been ironed out. The only situation in which he now barked was at times of perceived danger. But here, too, he had improved enormously.

One weekend, however, Tom couldn't help wondering why Dexter had been making woofing noises all morning. Saturdays were normally a quiet time in the neighbourhood, yet it was as if strangers were constantly coming near the front door or passing close by the boundary fence. When Tom took a look out of the window, he saw something hilarious. Dexter would run to the garden fence. He would then turn to the house and let out a short burst of barks. No sooner had he done so than a family member would appear with a piece of food reward, as thanks for the warning. The problem was that there were no threats at all. Watching from upstairs, Tom saw that the street was quiet. It has always been well known that boxers are highly intelligent. Even by the standards of his breed, Dexter was a very bright boxer indeed: he was inventing passers-by so that he could be rewarded with food.

When I heard this story, I quickly realised what had happened. In accordance with the method, Tom and his family had introduced the idea of thanking Dexter for his warning of a perceived danger. This is something we will cover in due course. The family had underlined the message by handing out food rewards. It was wonderful to see a family involved in this way; the only problem was that they had failed to ease off the rewards, and the dog had devised a clever way of capitalising on this.

The lesson here, then, is that food rewards must be reduced and replaced by verbal praise. Certainly by the third and fourth weeks, it should only be used when your dog has behaved exceptionally well in dealing with difficult or totally unfamiliar circumstances. Otherwise you will be conned in the same way as Dexter's owners were…

THE POWER OF PLAYTIME

The first forty-eight hours present a real challenge to both dog and owner. It is a time for concentration and discipline. But it is also a time when fun has its place too. The act of play is an enormously powerful tool for

building on the early successes of Amichien Bonding. This is a good time
to bring this into your armoury too. We can see how hugely important
play is when we again look at the model of the wolf pack. Wolves do not
go out for a casual walk in the way humans do. They only venture out
from the security of the den on two occasions: the hunt and when the den
and the pack as a whole are on the move, relocating their territory.

A wolf's major source of exercise and social activity comes through
play. This is something that every member of the pack takes part in. Even

Absent Friends
The two dogs who
taught me so much and
who I miss so badly:
Sasha (left) and Barmie.

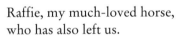

Raffie, my much-loved horse,
who has also left us.

Listening at Large

In 2001, Channel 5 in the UK broadcast *The Dog Listener*, a series of seven television programmes devoted to my work, in which I visited 'problem' dogs around the country. The following pages feature some of the colourful characters I encountered on my travels.

Spike's Progress: I have mentioned Spike, the nervous rescue dog who hated crossing bridges, in the main text. These pictures chart his progress in facing up to his phobia.

Top: TV presenter Mark Curry tries in vain to persuade Spike to walk with him.

Above: Spike's owners undergo the usual ritual of carrying him across the bridge.

Right: Problem solved: after being introduced to my method, Spike and his family, Jo, Paul and little Katie, take their first confident steps across the bridge.

Dogs Behaving Badly

Below are three lively
customers I encountered.

Pip and Peggy, a pair
of overexuberant
Weimaraners.

Fester, a supercharged
Chihuahua, poised to
launch herself at
Mark Curry.

Murphy, a delinquent Irish
wolfhound, bounds at another
presenter, Paul Hendy.

Common Complaints

Below, a trio of dogs demonstrate some of the problems I am regularly asked to tackle.

William shows the classic signs of anxiety as he chews a door.

Casper the Rottweiler and his friend Ben stare nervously out as their owner moves around outside the den: a textbook case of separation anxiety.

Gabby, a German shepherd-Border collie cross, whose owner had a hard time controlling her as she attacked other dogs.

Uncommon Complaints

Three less conventional dogs
I came across.

Zack, a German shepherd who
hated police uniforms, runs for
cover as his owner, a policeman,
returns home from work.

Charlie, a springer spaniel
who licked sunbeams
and hated shadows.

Hamish, the hyper-anxious
Jack Russell-Border collie
cross who chased his tail like
a whirling dervish.

Changed Characters

Max, a Border collie who hated going for walks, prepares to head off into the wide world with his owner Alison.

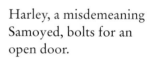

Harley, a misdemeaning Samoyed, bolts for an open door.

On the road to success: a much better behaved Harley is reunited after separating from his owner Andrea.

Bramble, a boxer who was a menace to society until I met him, behaves impeccably in his family home.

Benson, a highly nervous and aggressive St Bernard, squabbles with his fellow pack members.

One month later, after an introduction to Amichien Bonding, Benson and his pals relax in perfect harmony with each other and their disbelieving owners, Tansy and Andrew.

Family Album

There is still nothing more exhilarating than spending time with your best friends. A few images of me and my own dogs.

Top: Me playing ball with Sadie.
Top right: Molly running with a ball.
Above: Cuddling my springers.
Right: Rewarding my dogs for a job well done.

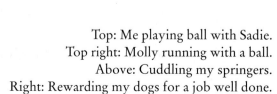

the Alphas enjoy a bit of rough-and-tumble – and they, once more, use it as a means of subtly re-emphasising their leadership. By ensuring they control playtime, the Alphas remain the decision-makers. They do so by retaining control of the whole situation, choosing the timing of play and exercising ownership of whatever objects might be used for the purposes of play. But, more subtly, by creating an atmosphere in which the entire pack enjoys itself, they are providing their pack members with yet another reason to value and appreciate the society they form together.

It is akin to the sort of bonding sessions so popular among large corporations these days. The idea there is that people get together outside of the work environment and have fun. The hierarchical order is not broken – the boss remains the boss – yet the staff's perception of the corporation is once more reinforced. They see it as a community that offers them enjoyment as well as security. Why would they want to undermine or move away from this?

Puppies, in particular, learn an incredible amount through play. It is by tumbling around and chewing and biting on playthings that they develop their athletic abilities and cut their teeth. Yet it is precisely because play holds such a potent power to pass on messages that it must, from the outset, be conducted in the right way. It is another occasion on which you must establish, and maintain, leadership.

I introduced the concept of 'toys not trophies' in my first book – it is worth reiterating again here, nevertheless. Again, it is an area best understood by considering it from the dog's point of view. As far as we are concerned, our everyday toys: balls, rag dolls, bones and throwing sticks, are nothing more than playthings. Yet, if we look at it from the dog's perspective, these objects take on a much greater significance. Within the natural environment, playtime is another crucial opportunity for the Alpha pair to underline their leadership status.

When we look at it from this angle, we immediately see why it is that dogs attach such importance to play. Far from being unimportant playthings, toys are trophies, badges of honour if you will, to be won and lost within the pack environment. It is something that becomes blindingly obvious when we see it in these terms. We have all seen the way packs of puppies wrestle around for toys. The triumphant dog struts around afterwards, like a heavyweight boxer with his vanquished opponent lying at his feet. I have also seen situations where dogs become agitated and aggressive because their owners will not play with them, when they are presented with a toy. People tend to dismiss this as playfulness, over-exuberance or childlike tantrum throwing. In fact, it is a control issue. Dogs believe they are in charge of playtime and behave accordingly. By allowing our pets to believe they have control of playtime and the all-important status symbols that are their toys, we are also allowing them to delude themselves about their place within the pack. This is why it is so important that you impose yourself as leader through play by applying the few simple principles below.

Take Control of the Toy Box

The most straightforward way of imposing leadership at playtime is by assuming control of the toys themselves. Now I am not, in any way, advocating that playtime is eliminated unless you are present: that would be silly and plain wrong. Therefore, I ask owners to leave one or two favourite toys around the house so that the dog can choose to play on its own. At the same time, I insist owners keep the toys used for interaction in a place where the dog cannot get access to them. By doing this, you make sure the potent power of playtime lies in your hands from the very beginning. It is you and you alone who decides when playtime takes place and which toys are used. As for the choice of toys, that is entirely a matter of personal choice. My only piece of advice here is to avoid small toys. Dogs have choked, and in some cases died, because owners have given them objects small enough to get trapped in their windpipes. You wouldn't leave a child to play with something that could choke it, so why would you think of doing any different with a dog?

Don't Get into Contests

As I have explained, to the dog play is never simply for play's sake. It is a contest that it wants to win, and this is an attitude that you should adopt too. For this reason, you should never get into tugging contests with your dog; by doing so, you are allowing it to dictate the rules of the game. At the same time, there is the danger of showing a dog – particularly a larger breed – that it has physical superiority over you. Needless to say, if a dog starts to believe it is stronger than its leader, it will begin to reassess whether that person should retain their status.

The same applies with play biting. Many owners have fun letting their puppies gnaw away at a finger, despite the nasty little nip the pup's young, needle-sharp teeth can inflict. If the biting is allowed to continue, however, you risk getting hurt and, once again, your dog stands to gain an inflated opinion of its status within the pack. This simply must not happen. If your puppy gets carried away and bites too hard, you must immediately remove your hand and end the playtime. The puppy must learn the consequences of this action.

Make Play Constructive

Playing with your dog is a magical part of the relationship, something to be cherished and enjoyed at all times. Given that my method is based around non-aggression, it is often the perfect time to transmit information to the dog. I frequently use play to practise and top up skills like the recall and coming to heel, which we shall come to later. Both of these skills need regular refreshing. I do this simply by moving away from my dogs when they retrieve and return to me with a ball. I then encourage them to come to me. They want the game to continue. They know that, for it to do so, the ball must be back in my hand; the dog wants to carry on playing so it behaves in a way that ensures this happens. Again, the simplest of signals can be the most powerful.

PART THREE:

DAYS 3–7

Why There's No Place Like Home

The first forty-eight hours are tough, I make no bones about that. But, by the third day, the benefits of all your hard work should begin to shine through. During the remainder of the first week, you can expect to make huge improvements in your ability to communicate with and control your dog. You should, for instance, be ready to develop your first set of basic control skills. You should also be able to move on to the third element of the method, dealing with times of perceived danger such as the introduction of unfamiliar faces and noises. Best of all, you should be able to have some real fun with your dog.

It will be an exciting and rewarding time for all owners. But it will also be a time when you must remain disciplined. To ensure this, I insist that this next phase is conducted within the confines of the home environment. If I have a single recurring message here, it is summed up best in the words of Dorothy in *The Wizard of Oz*: there really is no place like home. There are several reasons for this. Calmness and consistency are central to my method. In the frenzied world we live in, most people regard home as the one haven of sanity and peace where they can rely on finding these qualities. The upshot of this, of course, is that you are relaxed within this atmosphere. As I have explained, relaxation – keeping your head – is a key component to leadership as well. Home is the best place for this.

Home is the most potent place for your dog to learn too. Again, the parallel with the pack applies. It is only when the Alpha pair have led their charges safely back within their own marked ground that the mini society that is the pack can operate on every level. Outside this environment, life is defined by vigilance against attack and the rules of the hunt. At home the Alpha pair and their pack can eat, sleep, play and socialise more fully. It is here that the young learn the subtlest yet most powerful lessons about the way they are expected to live.

This stage is without doubt one of the hardest parts of my method for most owners. And I understand why. Their natural instincts, quite rightly, are to take their dog out into the wider world – to exercise. Some people say to me, 'It's unfair to the dog'; some even say it's cruel. My response is always the same: it is far more unfair and cruel to take a dog out into the world where neither the owner nor dog is capable of dealing with the dangers they are going to face there. I often compare learning my method with learning to drive a car. No one is allowed to take the wheel of a car until they are fully familiar with its controls and know how to operate them properly. No one in their right mind would go out on the road having learned to operate the accelerator and clutch, but having no idea where the brake is! It is no different with a dog. Anyone thinking of taking their dog out into the world before learning this is, to my mind, jumping in a car without the slightest idea how they are going to control, steer, or, most importantly, stop it. Lessons learned at home stay with a dog. Lessons learned away from home fade from the memory.

If I ever want to illustrate this point, I use the example of the troublesome pet I refer to as 'Dog X'! There have been times in the last few years when I've wondered whether I've walked accidentally into the plot of a John Le Carré spy novel. I've had to learn undercover skills that wouldn't go amiss within MI5. For reasons I can understand, some people do not like to admit publicly they have problems with their dogs. None of us is immune to criticism, and for many people their relationship with their dog is an intensely sensitive area. I usually encounter this sort of sensitivity when the job involves someone connected with the dog fraternity – and so it proved once more in this particular instance.

The owner's anxiety was made plain when I went to visit her and her handsome, tri-coloured Border collie at her home. As we talked at our initial meeting she actually said to me, 'If you see me in the streets please don't acknowledge me, walk on by.' It turned out that the lady was a very successful competitor within the obedience-class world. This is a very competitive world, owners travel the country and take pride in their performances. She had had success with other dogs and was a judge herself. People often ask me how I can square working with people who adhere to these ideas with my disdain for the very word 'obedience'. My answer is always the same. If there is a chance I can convert an owner to my compassionate method, it is worth taking.

The dog I was asked to look at was potentially one of the best the owner had ever worked with. But he had one flaw in the eyes of the judges. Obedience-class competitions are not dissimilar to the equestrian dressage contests. Owners are judged on their ability to manoeuvre their dogs according to precise instructions. This particular dog would stop when his owner said and he would turn with her. But, throughout the heel-work part of the routine, he would refuse to walk in the optimum position, staying two or three inches in front of her instead. He would also lean into her, again something that was losing marks. It was very frustrating for her: the dog was getting scored very highly in every area but when it came to this one area he lost points heavily. Judges would comment along the lines of 'If only it didn't lead in front.'

The owner couldn't understand why the dog had progressed to this point yet couldn't make that final step. It seemed such a small adjustment to make. To me it was pretty obvious why the dog was holding back. The lady was taking him to weekly obedience classes, held in halls and fields in the village nearby. The classes were using all the old-fashioned ideas: enforcement, choke chains and commands. My argument, of course, is that force is not going to change anything. That aside; the main reason the owner was failing was that she had not established leadership in the dog's eyes, and, crucially, she was not working in the right environment, the home. Again, the comparison with children is a good one. If they have been taught to behave in a certain way at home, they are unlikely to behave differently in someone else's home. Equally, if they have been allowed to run amok at home, the chances are they will do something similar when they are outside the home.

When I visited the lady at home, it was clear that Dog X believed he was the boss. He was hyperactive and charged around furiously when I arrived. The owner told me that sometimes during the walk, he would run off on his own and she would not be able to recall him. I explained the problem to her. While she was trying to get him to do things exactly as she wanted, the dog instinctively wanted to lead her. In the competition ring he gave every sign of being under her control. Yet the leaning and the walking a few inches in front represented his sole gestures of defiance. They were the dog's way of saying: 'Actually, I'm the one in charge here.'

I quickly established a rapport with the dog, then I took him into the garden after about an hour. I worked with the lady, using her commands. She was pleased with the results and, as I left, I felt confident she would get the improvement she was after in the competitive environment. I told her to keep her dog away from classes for a couple of weeks and to work on removing leadership responsibility from him in the meantime. She was clearly dedicated to improving the dog and set about her task.

Unsurprisingly, I did not hear from her again for a long time. It was only after the publication of my first book that I came across her – at a book signing. She came up to me smiling warmly yet still pretending she didn't know me. I happily went along with her charade. I was keen to hear how she had been doing and was delighted to hear that her dog had been doing fantastically well in his obedience competitions and had even competed at Cruft's. He had, as she had always hoped, turned into the best dog she had ever had. As she was leaving, the lady touched me on the arm and offered a last, mildly embarrassed smile. 'Forgive me, but I took all the credit,' she said.

PERCEIVED DANGER

Nothing is more unsettling than the sight of something unfamiliar in familiar surroundings: it is the principle that gave Alfred Hitchcock a

career. And it applies to dogs as much as it does to us, their human companions. The difference with dogs is that, as the assumed leaders of the domestic pack, they believe it is their responsibility to deal with such threats. Understandably, it is these situations that are often responsible for the most extreme behaviour.

Again it helps to take a dog's-eye view of this. Seen from the dog's perspective, even the most trivial domestic event takes on a sinister new perspective. Take the arrival of the morning mail: how would any of us react if we heard a strange noise preceded by the sight of strange objects being thrust through the entrance to our den? Or the sudden arrival of a plumber: how would we feel if we discovered a man we had never seen before walking into our house brandishing a collection of dangerous-looking objects? Precisely – we'd be petrified for our own safety. And if we believed it was our responsibility to guard the den and its occupants, we would be even more distressed.

The domestic home is a minefield of sights and sounds that could easily be construed as being potentially dangerous. Outside, there are the sounds of cars, lorries, aeroplanes and passers-by. Inside there are the assorted sounds of daily life, from washing machines and telephones to the bumps and bangs of young children crashing around in their rooms. The problem is that humans do not understand this. So, when they hear a dog barking at the sound of a ringing doorbell, they chastise it for being too noisy. When they see it lurching at a postman, they condemn it for its aggression. They fail to understand that, in reality, the dog is dutifully carrying out the leadership role for which it believes it has been elected. Is it any wonder when it proves so resistant to calls to 'Stop it' or 'Behave'? The dog is utterly confused that, rather than being congratulated, it is being abused by pack members who seem to have joined in the general panic. This is why you must learn to relieve your dog of this responsibility as early as possible within the process.

The true test of a good human leader lies in your ability to deal with times like these. The manner in which you deal with danger is of no less importance in the canine world. By taking charge of a situation, you can take a huge stride towards underlining your long-term suitability to lead the pack. And to achieve this, you must now build on the work you have already done in establishing yourself as the pack leader.

Dogs assimilate easily into domestic environments and – apart from some exceptions – learn to live with many everyday occurrences. Yet some dogs are sent into a blind panic by certain noises. The key to working in all these situations is, again, calmness, consistency and providing a convincing model of leadership. The dog must first be reminded of its status as a subordinate. It must then be reminded that this role does not require it to deal with the situation at hand.

The best way to illustrate this is by looking at the most common threat to the domestic pack: when outsiders enter the 'den'. Viewing the situation from the dog's perspective, it is easy to see why it gets so agitated. At the top of its job description is its responsibility to guard the den and all its members from invasion and attack. When it hears a knock on the door and then sees a stranger about to enter the house, the only logical conclusion, to the dog at least, is that an assault on the den is about to take place. Its territorial space is being invaded and it needs to do something to reclaim it. When we look at it in this way, it is little wonder that dogs bark, rush at, or even attack people when they arrive in the home.

How, then, should you deal with this potentially dangerous situation? The first time a visitor comes to your house, you must instantly establish the precedent that it is you who deals with the situation. If your dog simply barks or growls, you should step forward to greet the visitor and, at the same time, thank the dog for its help. You must make sure you do this calmly and quickly. You must never make something out of nothing and dramatise the situation. The effect here is twofold: by remaining calm, you are once more displaying all the credentials of a leader. At the same time, you are acknowledging the dog's help. Remember, even after its demotion from the role of leader, the dog's instincts are geared towards integrating itself into a happy and successful domestic pack. It wants to feel useful, that it is contributing. By listening to your dog, then telling it that it has contributed to defending the den, you are reassuring the dog about its importance as a pack member and your dog will feel good about this.

Of course, all dogs have different personalities. And some may react to perceived danger in more aggressive ways. If your dog does have a history or tendency towards being aggressive, it should be fitted with a collar during the early days, so that you are prepared for every eventuality. If your dog does leap up at a visitor, you must act decisively. The dog should be led away from the visitor by its collar. You should then guide the visitor into the house, and away from the dog. If your dog's behaviour is so aggressive that it fails to remain out of the way, you must remove it from the scene.

There is nothing for you to fear at this stage. It is important to remember that my method is a holistic approach. By the time you are fully conversant with it, you will be blitzing your dog with powerful signals that relieve it of its leadership. By the time your first visitor comes to the home, you will hopefully already have begun establishing a new hierarchical order and your dog should be more receptive to requests.

Of course, it is perfectly possible that a visitor may come to the house before you have had time to apply any other element of the method. No matter: your reaction to your dog should be the same, and it should be thanked for its help. The process will have been given a useful kick-start. If your dog does react to the arrival of a visitor, it is advisable that you pre-empt the same thing happening again on departure. The easiest way to do this is by removing your dog to another room or to the garden shortly before the visitor leaves. When you have the home to yourself again, you can bring the dog back in and go through the normal reuniting process. The beauty of this is that it will enable you to tackle immediately whatever short-term effect the stranger's arrival may have had.

The arrival of strangers is not the only situation in which a dog feels the pack is under threat. When a member of your family leaves the home, your dog feels equally challenged as leader. Again it is easy to see why this is when we think about it: the dog has no concept of time, in the human sense at least. So when it sees a member of the household – of the pack for which it believes it is responsible – heading through the door, it has no idea whether this person is ever going to return. It is no surprise that dogs become so agitated when family members leave the home: they are trying to prevent the pack breaking up forever.

Again, the way to disarm this potentially explosive situation is by underlining the recurring message that this is no longer the dog's responsibility. It no longer has to worry about these matters. The dog should be offered another warm 'Thank you' and led away from the exit door. Ideally, this should be done through using a food reward. The dog will make a positive association the next time this occurs. In cases where the dog offers greater resistance or aggression, you must remove it in the same way as earlier, either by the collar or – in extreme cases – by a lead. It must be taken into another room so that the person can leave.

If you own a very nervous dog, you must once again show particular patience. Rather than confronting visitors, such dogs may run away and hide. In extreme cases, they may wet themselves. The crucial thing here is to leave the dog alone. It has chosen the option to take flight, and this option must not be removed from it. As with reuniting after a separation, these dogs must be given time to overcome their nerves. They must be persuaded that human beings are not automatically associated with pain. They must be given time to heal, and time to learn at their own pace.

It is important here to be aware of the direction in which this element of my method is heading. I have seen this process happen so many times now that I have become accustomed to it, but it may seem difficult to deal with at first. I can assure you that, in time, your dog will learn to accept your leadership. The arrival of a stranger will be greeted with a minor reaction. And, in time, a simple 'Thank you' will return your dog to its usual relaxed state.

One of the most extreme cases I've encountered that involved perceived danger was Hamish, a lovely Jack Russell-Border collie cross I met at his owner, Sarah's, home in a small, northern Scottish village near Banff. Hamish had lived with Sarah, her husband and their children since he was six months old. Throughout his two years in the house, he had been unbelievably nervous about visitors, passers-by and, most of all, the sound of the telephone ringing. He would instantly become wild-eyed and start chasing his tail, spinning like a top as he did so.

Sarah was passionate about dogs. She worked as a dog walker for professional people in her area and was involved with the Good Citizen scheme, encouraging owners to teach their dogs to avoid antisocial behaviour. She knew how much Hamish was suffering at these times. She could feel his anxiety and pain – and was prepared to do anything to ease it.

In the two years since Hamish's arrival in her home, Sarah had employed a psychologist, a behaviourist and a specialist 'dog trainer'. She had also been drowned in well-meaning advice from friends and family. As a consequence, she had received some rather extreme remedies. The behaviourist's big idea was to fill a tin can with pebbles! The theory was that this would be used as a distraction whenever Hamish got agitated. Sarah would either shake it in his face or throw the tin on to the floor near Hamish in an attempt to take his mind off things. It hadn't worked, needless to say. (All it had done, in fact, was give poor Hamish another potential threat to get in a funk about!)

The 'dog trainer' – and I use these quotation marks deliberately – suggested Sarah shake Hamish by the scruff of his neck. She hadn't even attempted this. She loved her dog so much, she wouldn't dream of being aggressive or violent towards him. Finally, and perhaps most ludicrously of all, the psychologist had told her to shout at Hamish. Whenever he went into a spin, she was to place her face next to him and bawl him out. Goodness knows what she was supposed to say. Sarah had rejected this advice, too, just as she done with the suggestions that she should smack him with a newspaper and throw water over him: she simply wasn't going to indulge in bullying her dog into submission.

Sarah had read my book but had struggled to impose herself on the situations when Hamish became most agitated, during times of perceived danger. Her plight had somehow come to the attention of the production company behind my television programme. The format of the show involved me applying my method to a group of dogs with a variety of problems. It was a hugely enjoyable experience, not least because it introduced me to some of the more interesting canine characters I have come across. I should point out that, as is the rule with the cases I tackle on-screen, I had no prior warning about Hamish or his problems. I went into Sarah's home 'cold', as it were. It did not take long to see what the problem was, however. Within moments of my walking in, he became extremely agitated. He began to spin around in a really crazy fashion. Sarah was in tears as she explained that, in addition to this, he had this habit of biting his tail. She said that she thought he was beyond help.

Without speaking, I took hold of Hamish's collar and sat down on a sofa, with Hamish sitting on the floor alongside me. I wanted to just hold him gently there. I exerted no force whatsoever. If there was any pulling, it was coming from him. I could sense how deeply distressed this dog was: his body was absolutely rigid, there was not a fibre in him that wasn't jangling, and his eyes were wild. This was hardly a surprise, given that his living room was filled with myself, a cameraman, a sound engineer, a researcher and the television show's presenter, Paul Hendy.

I explained to Sarah that I was going to hold Hamish in this position until his body was relaxed. His reward would then come in the form of his release. At the same time, I asked everyone else in the room to remain quiet and still, and, most importantly, to avoid looking at or making eye contact with Hamish. I held him for maybe a minute or so. Eventually, I felt the tension begin to ebb away. When I felt his whole body relax, I let the collar go.

The next step was for Sarah to try this. She did so with good results. Soon after Hamish was released again, one of the crew made a tiny noise. Hamish immediately went into his whirling dervish routine. So I asked Sarah to take hold of him again: 'Every time he does this, this is what you must do,' I told her. Sarah was very emotional, but she could see we were making some progress. By the fourth time we went through this routine, we made a real breakthrough. Almost as soon as Sarah sat down with Hamish alongside her, he relaxed.

The next step was to set off the phone. By now, I had programmed Sarah's phone number into my mobile. No sooner had I triggered the ringing than Hamish once more freaked out. His behaviour this time was even worse than previously. At one point, he was sitting on the floor with the tip of his tail in his mouth, shaking uncontrollably. Again, I took the lead and brought him to sit alongside me. I then triggered the phone again and held him in position until he relaxed.

By the end of my time with Sarah, Hamish was doing well. Such was his anxiety, however, that I warned Sarah that it might take her months to totally relieve him of the stress. I asked her to strengthen the process when the phone rang by excluding Hamish from the house and leaving him in the garden. When she let him back into the house, I wanted her to go through the reuniting after a separation routine and the five-minute rule so that she could apply a double whammy of signalling.

I left Sarah's house at 4pm on Tuesday. At 9am on Friday morning, she called me at home. Once more she was in tears – this time of joy. 'It's stopped,' she said. As usual, I urged caution. But the more she told me, the more convinced I was that Hamish had finally been relieved of the burden of guarding the house. Sarah told me Hamish had slept a lot, a telltale sign of a dog that is recharging its batteries after a hugely emotional period. As we were talking on the phone, someone walked past the front window of Sarah's home. Seventy-two hours earlier, this would have sent Hamish into orbit. Sarah told me that, just like the previous evening when the phone rang, he had barely raised his head and had gone straight back to sleep. Days before, I'd warned Sarah that I didn't possess the power to change things like some fairy godmother. I told her she faced a long, hard road. Even I was amazed at how quickly things had changed. 'What was that you said about not having a magic wand?' she laughed.

PUSHING THE BOUNDARIES: PREPARING FOR THE WALK

By now, your dog should be comfortable within its new environment. It should be familiar with its sights and sounds, its household members, both human and canine. And, most importantly, it should have begun to understand its new, subordinate status within the hierarchy of its domestic pack. As it learns to relax, the next natural step will be for you and your dog to push the boundaries of this environment. Your dog will, understandably, want to explore the world more fully; I believe in taking every possibly opportunity to harness the dog's positive instincts. This therefore presents the perfect opportunity for you and your dog to move forward by laying the groundwork for those first steps into the wider world – and the day when you take your dog for its first walk.

Again, it is important to stress that all dogs must be treated as individuals and allowed to develop at their own pace. In general, I recommend that you wait seven days before actually venturing out. Some owners, however, will have to wait much longer before venturing out. The reason for this is simply that not all dogs will be capable of progressing this quickly. Rescue dogs with particularly nervous dispositions may have to wait up to a month before they are ready to venture back out into a world that has, after all, treated them appallingly in the past. Puppies, too, should not walk out into the wider world until they are three to four months old at least. I advocate keeping puppies away from any risk of infection until two weeks after their second vaccination – about fourteen weeks into their life. Well-organised puppy playgroups provide a useful means of socialising and providing play during this time.

For most dogs, however, key controls at home can begin from day three onwards. Many owners, I know, find it hard to wait this long to go out on a walk. But the key thing to remember here is that, once out in a strange and unfamiliar world, your dog is going to rely on its newly elected leader to guide it every step of the way. To be able to do this, you need to be able to control your dog via the lead. So the next four or five days must be spent introducing, developing and perfecting the key controls: the sit, heel work, the turn, the wait, the stay and the recall.

BASIC CONTROL 1: THE SIT

The sit is the cornerstone of an owner's repertoire of controls. It will be a fundamental part of life, particularly useful when doing things like grooming, administering medicine or fitting the lead before the walk. It is vital, then, that this primary and most basic technique should begin during the key, first phase of the training.

Step 1

You want your dog to make a positive association with the act of sitting. To do this, take a piece of food, show it to the dog, then bring it toward and over its head. As you do this, slowly say the word 'Sit'.

Step 2

As the dog follows the food with its eyes, it should arch its neck backwards, so that its whole body tips back and it eventually ends up sitting down.

Step 3

The dog should be rewarded with warm praise, maybe some smoothing of the head and, of course, the right to eat the morsel from your hand. This should be done as soon as the dog's bottom touches the ground, so it knows that the word 'Sit', its action and the ensuing reward are inextricably linked.

Use this technique sparingly at first. Don't, for instance, ask your dog to sit each time you ask it to come to you. There is a good reason for this: remember, dogs are deeply manipulative creatures, and they also know when they are on to a good thing. Remember, once a dog has grasped a principle, it may try to manipulate you into repeating the process again and again. I have seen dogs sit there, staring angelically at their owners, expecting a reward each time. It is vital that this does not happen, as the object of the exercise is to underline your status as leader. The dog is not going to grasp this if it is able to influence when food reward is dispensed. Only the leader should decide this.

FREQUENTLY ASKED QUESTIONS

What If My Dog Doesn't Respond?

Dogs are not mind-readers so you cannot expect them to understand what you want immediately. If at you don't succeed, try again: it may take several attempts to get this right, but you must remain calm.

When I Move the Food over My Dog's Head, It Shuffles Backwards on All Fours.
Move to a wall or a closed door. Place your dog with its back to the wall or door. It cannot now move backwards and should tip onto its bottom when the process is repeated. Again, success may take time, but your dog will not need teaching a second time.

What If My Dog Still Refuses to Sit?

Gently place a hand behind your dog. The hand should only touch its bottom ever so lightly, in the way a baby is supported before it learns to sit up unaided. Force has no part in my method: the hand is only there as a stop. Pass the food over the dog's head again, repeating until it tips over and sits of its own free will.

BASIC CONTROL 2: HEEL WORK

No one wants to go for a walk with a dog that is trying to pull your arms out of their sockets. No one wants to go for a walk with a dog that is panting and being dragged along like a reluctant conscript. It is a misery for everybody concerned; there is no joy in it. So the goal here is to train your dog to walk closely by your side at all times, and to do so happily on the end of a lead. The dog should slow down, speed up and stop in harmony with you. As before, this is something that should be developed in slow but steady stages.

Step 1
The first thing you must do is elect the side you want your dog to walk on. Most people prefer their dog to walk on their left. I know that within the gun-dog fraternity this is something that is encouraged because most people are right-handed and it leaves the right arm free. There is absolutely nothing wrong with training your dog to walk on the right. The key thing is that, once the decision is made, you stick to it. In what follows, I am assuming you want your dog to walk to the left. If you would prefer to have your dog on the right, simply reverse the instructions as appropriate.

Step 2
To begin heel work, you should work in a garden, a corridor or a room with sufficient space for you to walk a dozen or so paces to begin with. This should also be done without the use of a lead. It is vital at this stage that your dog retains the option of flight: to deny it may result in aggression.

You should first turn your back on your dog, making sure as you do so that you have a piece of food reward ready. Put the food in your left hand and bring it down along the side of your leg until it reaches a height equivalent to the dog's nose level. As you are doing this, you should call the dog's name and request it to 'Heel'. The presence of the food reward

should bring your dog to your side. If it approaches as requested, your dog should be given the reward and praised warmly.

Of course, this is something that may take a time to get right. If, for instance, your dog is attracted by the smell of the food and arrives at your side uninvited, then it must be ignored for a few minutes. The routine must then be started again. Similarly, if your dog does not appear, the exercise should be abandoned and tried again at least an hour later. There should be no interaction between you and your dog during this cut-off period.

Step 3

You must now begin walking slowly. If your dog remains in position at your side for the length of the walk, it should again be rewarded and praised at the end. It is vital to remember again at this point that your dog is not a mind-reader: it is up to you to speak its language. So, if it wanders slightly away from you, you should encourage it to return to the correct position by the use of a positive association. A supply of food reward

should be ready again. The dog should be reminded to 'Heel' once more. Again, the key thing, as always, is that you remain calm, that your pulse rate remains low. If your dog does not get it right immediately, be patient and keep repeating the exercise.

If your dog becomes agitated or loses interest and starts jumping around, the exercise should be abandoned and again there should be no interaction for at least an hour. Neither humans nor dogs are capable of digesting important information when they are in an agitated state, so allow things to calm down and start again later.

Step 4

As your dog learns to walk in harmony with you, the length, speed and direction of the walk should be changed. You should stop and start again occasionally, using a few, softly spoken words so as to gain the dog's maximum attention. In the outside world, you and your dog will have to negotiate all sorts of routes, and this is vital preparation for the day when you face this test together for the first time.

Introducing the Lead

An observer watching a dog that has learned to walk to heel in the right way might well imagine it is connected to its owner by an invisible line. The next stage of the process is to add a visible line in the form of a lead. In most respects this is the same as the heel routine above.

Step 1

Bring your dog to heel. As it stands at your side, you should place the lead gently and without fuss over the dog's head.

Step 2

You should now begin walking, encouraging your dog to stay at your side as normal. If the dog begins pulling on the lead, you should stop and calmly stand your ground. Do not get into a tugging match with the dog: the lead is not a weapon to be used to jerk or yank an animal around with. The dog should be asked to once more come to heel. If the groundwork has been done properly, your dog should return to its starting position easily. The walk should then be resumed once more, with you rewarding the dog each time it successfully completes its length without your pulling and calling it back to heel each time it tugs on the lead.

Step 3

You should slowly extend the length of the walk you take, using the available space to its maximum effect. As you develop this skill, you should become less and less aware of the lead even existing.

BASIC CONTROL 3: THE TURN

It is a very rare walk indeed that heads in a single, straight line all the way. It is therefore going to be vital that you learn to make turns using the lead. These, again, are manoeuvres that can be practised and perfected at home.

Again, I am assuming here that most people will walk with their dog to the left. If, however, it is the right, simply reverse the instructions.

Turning Right

As you pivot round, you should lead with your right leg. Leading with the left leg will cause all sorts of problems: the dog will be blocked from turning right and you and your dog run the serious risk of tripping over each other. As you turn, use a distinctive word that your dog will always associate with this manoeuvre from now on. You are free to use whatever word you like, but the traditional word in the dog world is 'Close'. The most important thing is that your word has a distinctive sound.

As you turn your body, your dog's head will move with the lead and its body should angle around to the right as well. This is something that should happen instinctively. If you have applied all that has gone before properly, your dog should by now be paying attention to you at all times, and it should want to be with you at all times too. The dog should be doing these things of its own free will.

Turning Left

This is a slightly more complex manoeuvre, so I advise you to begin by gathering up your lead so that there is no slack. This should ensure that the dog is at your side as you prepare to make the turn. You should extend your left leg out as far as you can ahead of you. At this point, your leg should be touching the dog's neck area. Again, you should choose a word to be associated with this control; the traditional word is 'Back', for the simple reason that the dog is being asked to drop back.

As you pivot left, your dog should naturally drop back. And because your body is now gently applying pressure to your dog's body, the dog should turn naturally to the left with you. The key here, as always, is that there is nothing sudden or violent about this. It should happen smoothly, seamlessly and calmly, with plenty of warm praise when things go well. Soon the dog should be reacting naturally to the movements of your legs.

Turning Right: Stages 1–4

Turning Left: Stages 1–4

BASIC CONTROL 4: THE WAIT

The ability to bring a dog to an instant halt is vital – both on and off lead. It is important, then, that a new instruction, the wait, is introduced at this time. It is done simply enough – as you develop heel work, you should introduce sudden stops accompanied by the short, sharp but non-threatening instruction: 'Wait'. After a brief few moments you should get on your way again, using the instruction 'Heel'. Once more, there is a strong case for using food reward as a means of getting this control right. This may be one of the most important lessons your dog will learn, and it should carry positive associations from the outset.

Dual Controls

I am certainly not an advocate of gadgetry: my aim is to replicate as much as possible the sort of natural behaviour found in the wild. And when did anyone ever see a wolf using a clicker to teach one of its cubs how to behave? In the real world, however, there has to be an element of flexibility and I accept that, for some people, controlling a lively dog in the early stages is going to be a difficult process. In the case of rescue dogs that have a history of bolting after cars, jumping at or attacking people, or simply running off, this is not something that can be left to chance.

For this reason, I advocate that in some instances owners use what I call 'dual controls' and, in addition to the collar and lead, they use a head brace. Each is controlled from a separate hand, giving you twin means of managing your dog. If the dog has a habit of suddenly swinging its head around, the head brace can be used to bring it back into position. This is only a temporary measure, hopefully. Once the dog has got the message, the head brace should be discarded.

BASIC CONTROL 5: THE STAY AND THE RECALL

You and your dog will step into a world full of dangers. It is therefore vital that you are able to freeze the dog in its tracks at any hint of danger. Equally important, you must be able to call it back to you, wherever it is. Therefore you must master two new controls here, the stay and the recall. In essence these are extensions of the sit and the come.

Step 1
Ask the dog to come and then sit. By now these should both be instinctive for it. You and your dog should now be facing each other. Take one step back and, as your weight is transferred to your back leg, extend an arm and place the flat of your hand about one foot in front of the dog's face. At the same time, softly say: 'Stay'.

Step 2
Complete the transfer of weight so that there is now one stride separating you from your dog. If the dog comes to close the gap, your weight should be transferred back onto the front foot. Your dog should again be asked to sit on the original spot. If necessary, gently place your hand on its chest to position it there. Repeat the move of earlier. It will not take the dog long to realise you are not running away and it will stay.

Step 3
When you can stand with both your feet together one step away, you should stand for a few seconds and return to the dog and reward it with praise. By this stage, any food reward should be less necessary.

Step 4
The previous routine should now be practised with you moving back to a distance of two strides away from the dog. Again, if the dog comes, or even begins to fidget or raise its bottom in advance of a move, you should quickly move back to the dog and repeat the sit instruction.

Step 5

Once you are standing successfully two steps away, your dog should be asked to come. It should be rewarded with food at this point: it has made an important step forward. The sit and come routines have successfully evolved into the stay and recall.

Step 6

This should be extended until your dog stays for thirty seconds and you can turn away from it without the dog moving towards you. If it does make a move, turn back and repeat the stay command.

GROOMING

A dog is a source of great pride for most owners. Many spend long hours, not to mention large chunks of their hard-earned income, ensuring their pets look their best. Yet this area can be fraught with problems. I have come across cases where behavioural problems with dogs have prevented owners from grooming them, sometimes for weeks or even months. This, clearly, is a situation that no owner can allow to go untreated.

Once more, it is helpful to view this at first from the dog's perspective. To the dog, like the wolf, decisions regarding where, when and with whom it does its grooming are closely associated with leadership. Within a wolf pack, the Alpha pair help groom and clean each other. It is not uncommon for subordinate pack members to play a role, too, licking their leaders clean – but only when invited to do so. Given this, then, it is easy to see why dogs can be so sensitive to the idea of their owners running a brush through their hair uninvited.

The story of a tiny Yorkshire terrier called Bobby illustrates how extreme the problem can be – and how it can be overcome. Bobby lived with his owner, Mrs Pearce, in a village a short drive from my home. Bobby was a very nervous dog: he was terrified of leaving the house, barked at visitors and was capable of nipping at anyone who came too close for his comfort.

It was his biting that prompted Mrs Pearce to call me. But it was during my first visit that I learned the extent of her grooming problems. Mrs Pearce told me that she could not go anywhere near Bobby with a brush. A Yorkshire terrier's coat grows quite long and needs regular attention. Out of desperation she had been forced to go through a routine whereby, every two months or so, Bobby was sedated by a vet before having his entire coat clipped off by a professional dog groomer. There were, of course, all sorts of reasons why this could not continue, not least the fact that a dog should not be given anaesthesia on such a regular basis.

During my visit, it was clear that Bobby was a very anxious dog. When

I arrived, he scampered at me, stopping at my feet and barking for all he was worth. It took a little while to exhaust his repertoire. Once he had calmed down, I made the first step towards easing Mrs Pearce's problems. After observing the five-minute rule, I asked Bobby to come to me. At the same time, I placed Mrs Pearce's grooming brush on the floor, about six inches in front of me. Bobby recoiled at first but came back towards me when I called him a second time. It was important at this point that he knew he had the flight option available to him. Eventually, he approached the brush and me.

By this time, I had been working with Bobby for an hour and a half. I knew I was not going to make more progress with the brushing in one day, so I asked Mrs Pearce to incorporate a plan to introduce grooming into the thirty-day programme ahead of her. This was not the first such case I have come across, and nor will it be the last. Rescue dogs in particular can be incredibly wary of anyone laying a hand, let alone a brush, on them. Whenever I work with a dog such as this, I slowly encourage them to approach their owner so that the owner can introduce a brush across their body without them recoiling or snapping. This is what I asked of Mrs Pearce. Each day, I wanted her to encourage Bobby to take a step closer to the brush. I told her not to rush. As ever, I emphasised the need to first present herself as a convincing and decisive leader; but at all times, too, she had to allow Bobby the option of flight.

When I spoke to Mrs Pearce ten days into the method, she had progressed to such an extent that she could now hold the brush in her hand when Bobby came to her. At that stage, she did not yet feel confident enough to try stroking him with the brush, however. By the time she had begun the third week, she had crossed this hurdle and had begun to run the brush, very gently, across Bobby's chest.

Of course, this work wasn't going on in isolation. Mrs Pearce was bombarding Bobby with signals from all the other elements of the method. Nowadays, Bobby can have a haircut without any kind of sedation. And Mrs Pearce grooms him at home herself. The bond between the two of them has grown deeper than ever – all thanks to the patience and understanding both showed when it was needed.

FREQUENTLY ASKED QUESTIONS

Can I Groom a Pack Together?

My answer to this often-asked question is no. In my experience, it is far better to groom members of a pack of dogs separately. This is partly sentimental in a way: to me, grooming is an enjoyable and intimate part of an owner's relationship with their dog. It builds a bond between the two. But more importantly, by separating your dogs, you avoid the possibility of giving out dangerous signals regarding one dog's status.

This can happen in two ways, firstly by grooming – and thereby seeming to favour – one dog ahead of another. But it can also happen if you raise dogs onto tables for grooming. One only has to look at dogs that jump up to understand the importance of height within the canine mindset. Dogs that jump are, of course, trying to gain equal status with their owner. So it follows that, if a pack is brought into a room to be groomed together, the sight of one dog being raised above the rest transmits a potentially explosive message. It is signalling that this dog is being elevated in status. As a result, when the dog is lowered back to ground level it is almost certain to be challenged by canine peers who are suddenly uncertain of its place within their pack. In my view the best, and simplest, way to avoid this is to keep the dogs separated. It will make for a more enjoyable and trouble-free time all round.

PART FOUR:
DAYS 8–14

Home and Away

What is about to happen is an extremely significant moment in the relatively short history of the pack in its present hierarchical form. The family is about to step out of its den into the wider world. It is important at this stage to go back to first principles, and to once more imagine this situation from the dog's perspective. For the dog, exiting the den can only mean one thing is happening: it is heading off on the hunt.

Within the wolf pack, this is a time when the Alpha pair, from the outset, stamp their authority on their subordinates. It is the Alpha pair that decide when the hunt occurs; it is the Alpha pair that check to see whether it is safe to leave the den; and it is the Alpha pair that lead the pack into the outside world and choose the direction in which they are to head.

It is vital that, each time the pack goes out on the walk, you take charge of each of these aspects. And it is now that all the groundwork of the previous seven days should pay dividends. By now, you should have clearly demonstrated yourself as leader. And your dog or dogs should have consented to this and agreed to join this newly formed pack. Your dog will have learned it has no reason to fear for itself when you are in charge. It should now be willing to follow you out into the wider world and to face whatever is waiting for it there. All in all then, the big day has finally arrived.

135

THE WALK

Step 1

Call your dog to you, pop on the lead and get it to walk to heel with you to the door. If the dog gets overexcited or rushes ahead of you, calm things down by holding your ground. If necessary, postpone the whole event if your dog misbehaves: it will quickly get the message.

Step 2

The crucial thing now is that you are the first person to cross the threshold. If your dog tries to move forward and get out ahead of you, you should step back and bring it to heel. As usual, this should be done calmly, without any histrionics or raised voices. You should then head off again, once more leading the way through the door.

Step 3

Once outside, your dog should walk to heel. Don't worry too much if it gets a step or two ahead; you should only act if there is any tension on the lead, again calling the dog to heel. Each time your dog returns to its proper position, reward it with quiet, sincere praise.

Step 4

The next crucial moment comes when you and your dog reach the boundary of your home. It is imperative here that you reinforce your leadership by choosing the direction the walk takes. So, if your dog begins heading off in one direction, execute a smart about turn and start walking the other way. If your dog veers off again, you should turn once more. Repeat this until the dog understands that it is not in charge of the walk. Again, the key thing here is that no words are spoken. Your dog must be made to voluntarily think: 'Where are we going?' It should then come to the conclusion that it is not up to it to decide, and it should follow you, its leader, of its own free will.

The first walk should be a gentle introduction for both you and the dog, and it should continue this way for the next few days. You should build up your confidence with the controls you have developed so far. Your dog should become used to the idea that, when it steps out into the world with you, it always returns safely home. At this point, I do not recommend you let your dog off its lead. The consequences of rushing into this could be dire: the dog might panic, bolt and do itself terrible damage. Patience, as ever, is a virtue. Apart from anything else, both you and your dog should take the time to enjoy this wonderful experience. There is immense joy to be had in leading a dog that is light on its feet, wagging its tail and happily exploring the exciting new world that is opening up around it.

It is also important for both you and your dog to enjoy yourselves. The whole point of my method is that you both learn to live with each other in a happy, pressure-free way. Every walk does not have to be a route march; you should let your dogs enjoy the scenery too. I would also caution people with dogs under a year old to be careful not to over-exercise them. Walking, particularly on hard surfaces like roads or pavements, can put pressure on growing bones and joints; most agility classes do not accept dogs under the age of eighteen months, as dogs are still growing at this age. By this stage, both you and your dog have come a long way, and you should both take some time to stop and smell the roses.

Pack-Walking

A good owner should never take their leadership of the pack for granted. Even after successfully establishing yourself as leader, you must be aware that this status is going to be challenged on a regular basis. Just like any good chief executive of a company, you must be aware of the individuals you manage, and should know the forces that operate between them. If you own a pack containing two or more dogs, you must always remain aware of the dynamics within that pack. If, for instance, there are males and females, you must be ready for the females to come into season. This is a time when the dog's instincts are at its most highly tuned: along with survival, reproduction is the most important part of a dog's life.

Similarly, as your dogs grow older, you must be aware of the ever-shifting changes within the pack. I am often asked to deal with situations where a young dog is taking control from an older dog. My honest reply in these cases is that there is little I can do: a dog's nature has to be allowed to express itself. But, provided the dog believes its owner is leader, the changes will be assimilated without any harm coming to anyone. Just as parents can never choose their children's friends, so it is beyond you to control the alliances and friendships that form within your pack. All you can do is temper the behaviour within that pack by exerting strong, clear and compassionate leadership. And that leadership will never be more necessary than when the pack first go out for a walk together.

It is worth stating here that walking a large pack is a very skilled and possibly dangerous thing to do. If there are strong rivalries and person-alities within the pack, it is easy to inadvertently engineer a situation where a fight breaks out. If you fail to deal with this situation, the pack will have succeeded in exposing a frailty in your leadership, and all the hard work that has gone into establishing leadership will have been for nought. For this reason, I do not recommend that you take out a pack of more than four dogs unless you are highly skilled and experienced in looking after them.

Preparing a Pack for the Walk

Given the potential pitfalls of taking a pack out en masse, the build-up to this point must be gradual. You must begin the process with a series of one-on-one sessions with the pack members. Each should be taken out on a short walk to develop its individual relationship with you. As I have mentioned before, you must be extra careful when returning to the home with each dog. This will be the first moment two dogs have reunited after a separation since the new method was introduced, and it is highly unusual for the pack to be split up. The dog or dogs that have remained at home will go into a repertoire with the dog that has been outside. This can be a time of aggression, so I recommend the dogs are reunited one at a time – always ensuring there is never one dog on its own.

When each of the dogs has been out and has responded well to you, preparations can go ahead for the first pack walk. This will be a vital test of your leadership. It is a time to exhibit the strong, silent and decisive body language that your dogs now expect. This will be particularly important as the leads are being placed around your dogs' necks. It is in a dog's nature to get extremely agitated and excited at this point. It regards this, after all, as preparing to go on a hunt, and therefore needs to get its adrenaline pumping. Your job is to remain calm and to provide the cool, decisive leadership expected of you.

There should be no move towards the door until the entire pack has calmed down. If your dogs do not do this, you should exercise the ultimate sanction by removing the leads and thus signalling to the dogs that the walk has been cancelled. Provided your dogs do calm down, you should head off to the door, ensuring that – as with a solo dog – you, the leader, are the first across the threshold.

Pack Controls

In almost all respects, the preparation and execution of the walk is the same regardless of whether you have one or more dogs. There is, however, one extra control that will be required: the group heel. Obviously, it is simply not possible for every member of the pack to walk tightly to your heel – not without both you and your dogs tripping over each other, that is! You therefore need to develop a request that brings all the dogs into a tight formation at your side. I personally use the phrase 'Come in' or, sometimes, 'Together'. Again, this is something that can be practised at home, prior to the first walk. You should immediately reward those dogs that come to your side correctly, both as a positive association for them and as a negative one for those who have not responded.

The positions your dogs adopt will vary each time the walk is under-way. The key thing is that they come together immediately when you issue the instruction. If one dog is spoiling the walk for the rest, you should take the miscreant home, release him from his lead and leave him there. The remaining dogs should then set off with you again. The dog that has been banished will quickly get the message.

Of course, some dogs – particularly rescue dogs – may be unable to enjoy a walk due to some past trauma in their lives. One such dog, Spike the aqua-phobic walker, came to my attention through my television programme. Spike lived with his owners: Jo, Paul and their daughter Katie, in North Yorkshire. They had taken him in from a rescue centre. Like so many rescue dogs, he had a range of problems. What made Spike unique, however, was his dislike of crossing over water. The family lived near the coast and loved walking on the pier. They also lived near a river and several bridges. Spike would not cross any of them.

The moment I met him, it was clear to me that Spike was a dog utterly stressed at being the leader of his pack; his eyes were bulging out and, during my initial spell with him, he tried to leap all over me. He was a strong dog and I had to hold him in position at one point.

An owner is never going to understand all the elements of their dog's psychology. Where the roots of Spike's phobia lay, it was impossible to tell. I have come across dogs that have been so traumatised by certain events that they could not face any situation that reminded them of their past. In my first book, for instance, I wrote about a dog that had been found at the side of a motorway, having seemingly been thrown out of a speeding car. It was little wonder he had a phobia about travelling in cars. Perhaps, then, Spike had suffered a waterside experience that had scarred him mentally in the same way. Perhaps he had been thrown into a river? Perhaps he associated bridges with this? I was not going to be able to answer these questions. What I did know, however, was that, by releasing Spike from the responsibility of leadership, I would be able to help him overcome this fear.

I left the family to put the principles of Amichien Bonding into practice. Spike proved a fairly tough nut to crack. At one point, when Jo called him to her, Spike not only ignored her request but looked her in the eyes and deliberately urinated on his blanket. Jo called me in a bemused state about this. I explained that this was his way of challenging her, of testing her authority. I told her to take the blanket away, and to leave him to sleep on the bed without it that night. He had to be taught the consequences of his actions.

By the end of the second week, Spike had begun responding well. Jo and Paul started to take him out for short walks. They lived in a small, picturesque village with a pond, and Spike's phobia was such that he couldn't bear to go close to the pond. Now, I asked his owners to start walking near the water, whilst always making sure that they remained between Spike and the pond as they did so.

The first day, Jo and Paul walked a fair distance away from the pond. As it loomed into view, Spike glanced apprehensively towards the water. Jo rewarded him with a tidbit and some warm praise and continued walking. Over the next four days, they took the walk ever closer to the edge of the pond. Spike was wary but went along with them; the confidence in their leadership built up in the home was paying off. Day by day, Jo and Paul were demonstrating to Spike that he was always one hundred per cent safe at their sides. After a few days, Spike was walking on the pond side of Jo and Paul. The first breakthrough in his water phobia had appeared.

Spike's biggest test still remained. Twenty-three days after his owners had begun the method, they came to the moment of truth: the crossing of a bridge. The bridge they chose was near their home. As if there was not enough pressure on Jo, Paul and Katie, the television cameras were there to record the event. As if this challenge was not great enough, there had been torrential rain in the days before, and, as a result, the river's levels were extremely high and the water was travelling far faster than normal.

Jo and Paul were very apprehensive as they walked up the ramp leading to the bridge itself. As the cameras rolled, they reached the beginning of the bridge, but would Spike agree to cross it with them? For a second or so, the signs were not good. Spike put his first paw on the bridge and hesitated. Fortunately, Jo was alert and led him on immediately. Spike looked up at his owner for reassurance and moved on. That was his last moment of hesitation: to everyone's delight, Spike strolled across the bridge without any trouble at all. He looked totally unconcerned. The relief all around was immense – not least for me.

The programme director was eager to get a variety of shots of Spike's moment of glory and asked Paul and Jo to try leading him across again. Spike trotted across the bridge as before, and kept on doing so again and again for the benefit of the cameras. At one point, he even stopped in the middle of the bridge with his owners and stood there, staring at the raging waters below him: talk about a transformation! By the end of the afternoon, Jo and Paul were sick of the sight of the bridge. And happily exhausted with it.

PART FIVE:
DAYS 15-21

Off the Leash

Owners often ask me what their goal should be: what, in an ideal world, they should expect from their dog. My answer to this is always the same. All an owner should want from their dog is, firstly, that it stays with them of its own free will and, secondly, that the dog should do as they ask but, again, of its own free will. This is the point you should now have reached through following my method. If this is the case, the beginning of the third week will represent a significant landmark for both you and your dog. The quiet but nevertheless dramatic revolution that saw your dog deposed as leader is behind you. Now you can look forward to developing a deeper and more enjoyable life together. More work lies ahead of you, but it is now time to relax and enjoy each other's company.

In many ways, the next stage of the method marks a loosening of the ties that have bound you in the first weeks. The highlight of this period will come when your dog takes its first walks off the lead and begins to explore the world on its own. Even before that eventful moment arrives, you can slacken the reins slightly here and there.

It is important that, at this stage, you feel happy and in control. Just as importantly, your dog must be allowed to progress at its own pace, and the worst possible thing you can do is to rush things. It would, for instance, be wrong to move on to the next stage with a rescue dog if it still cowers in corners or recoils at times of danger: the dog clearly does not yet believe it is safe.

My method, as you know, contains principles that must be incorporated permanently into your lifestyle. Most importantly, for as long as you and your dog are together, you must always reinforce your leadership when reuniting, as well as at times of danger and on the walk. Your behaviour in these three fundamental situations will, slowly but surely, become as automatic as jumping into a car and driving down the road; you will become unaware that you are practising it. When you reach this stage, you can think about eliminating the fourth pillar of my method, gesture eating, from your routine.

At this point I should stress that, before doing this, you must be satisfied that your dog has achieved the crucial breakthroughs of the first fortnight. The dog should have progressed to the point where:

- It behaves well at feeding time
- It responds well to all requests while walking on the lead
- It accepts its owner's leadership when visitors arrive at the home
- It has significantly reduced its repertoire when reuniting
- It is generally a relaxed and happy dog

Certain principles should, of course, remain in place when it comes to mealtimes. The relaxation of the gesture-eating rule is not a charter for bad behaviour or bad eating habits. Under no circumstances should you now leave food on the floor at all times. And if your dog walks away from its meal, that meal must still be removed immediately. Dogs are always looking for chinks in their leader's armour, and you must remain vigilant in maintaining your control of mealtime.

By now, you should know your dog well enough to read his behaviour patterns. And if at any time you sense your dog slipping in its discipline, it is the easiest thing in the world to reintroduce the old routine. Gesture eating will always remain a powerful back-up tool for you when you wish to tighten up on your controls.

At the same time as you slacken the reins, you can also begin to be a little more relaxed about showing affection towards your dog. This, I know, always comes as a relief to those owners who feel somehow guilty for not fussing over their dogs during the early days of this method. It is important to state that I am not condoning a return to the situation where a dog comes bounding up uninvited onto an owner's lap. But, if your dog slides up alongside you or under your feet, as you relax watching TV or reading in the evening, there is nothing wrong with your now stroking it. Again, if the dog shows signs of disregarding your leadership, you can simply return to the old routine. Central to everything is a sense of flexibility. As long as you continue to be alert and open-minded about what is going on around you, you should be able to think your way through any situation that presents itself from now on.

FREEDOM: FIRST TIME OFF-LEAD

One of the purest pleasures of dog ownership comes when your dog is released to run free for the first time. The sight of a dog liberated to express its personality, athleticism and natural exuberance never fails to bring a smile to my face. I have spent much of my life trying to help dogs lead lives more in tune with their natural instincts; here they are truly in their element. This is a key moment after all your hard work. If the first steps into your garden were the kindergarten, primary school was your first walk in the outside world, and secondary school was your first walk in the park on the lead. This is when you graduate.

As ever, you must exercise common sense and patience here. Your dog should always remain on the lead in built-up areas or near roads; many people fail to realise the intrinsic danger of letting a dog run free in such hazardous situations. Once in open space, however, your dog can be readied for release. The first time this is attempted, I recommend you go through a routine that once more underlines the principles established at home. The journey leading up to this moment has been a long and demanding one. It is this moment, however, that should pay back the dividends.

'Go Play'

Once more, preparation is important, so choose a place that is quiet, somewhere like a large local park. The key thing is to find a little isolation. When it is clear there are no major distractions such as other dogs or large groups of people, bring the walk to a halt as usual.

Step 1
Get your dog to wait and remove its lead. Then walk with your dog at heel for a short distance, say twenty paces or so.

Step 2

Release your dog with a new instruction, such as 'Go play'. Be assured that this is the one instruction that will never need repeating; your dog will seize the opportunity with glee.

Step 3

Leave your dog to do its own thing for a while. Do not, however, let it stray too far, as this exercise is about building short-range control. When your dog is about ten yards away, ask him to come to you. Reward him with a tidbit of food when he comes.

Build up this work by increasing the distances to twenty, thirty and finally forty yards. I do not recommend letting the dog more than forty yards away in any circumstance. Experience has taught me that this is the outer limit of the dog's comfort zone, and beyond this distance there is a loss of control. If anything unforeseen happens, you will be too isolated and may be out of your dog's hearing range. In case of incidents like this, where the dog may fail to hear your voice, I recommend you carry an ordinary whistle.

This is another moment to truly enjoy your relationship with your dog. Both you and your dog should be exhilarated by the sheer joy of running free. You can add to your dog's positive association with this moment even more by playing with it; there is no more powerful a moment. Show it that freedom is great, but that enjoying that freedom interacting with its leader is even greater.

Releasing the Pack

As with an individual dog, if you own a pack, you should ask them to wait after slipping them off their leashes. You should then ask them to

walk closely together with you, before releasing them to 'Go play'. Again, it is important to apply your knowledge of the pack dynamic here. If there is a dominant figure within the pack, you should make sure this dog does not wander too far. The most effective way to do this is by working the dog hard through play and regular requests to come to you. By keeping this dominant dog within a safe and controllable distance, you will ensure the rest of your pack remains in close proximity too. If you work your dominant dog hard at the beginning of the walk in particular, you can pre-empt having to watch it too closely later on.

It is very easy for an owner to find they are dictated to by their pack. Wherever I go for a walk with my dogs, I see owners who are afraid to relax, and who watch their dogs like hawks; the joy of the walk seems to have been lost. Of course, you must keep a watchful eye on your dogs, but it does not have to be such a strain. To my mind, it is far more relaxing all round if it is the dogs who are constantly keeping half an eye on your every move, rather than vice versa. And this is what I ask all owners to do.

The best way to establish this is to walk in a different direction from the dogs the moment they are released to play. You should remain calm, almost aloof, when you do this. When your dogs come, you should react as if this was inevitable, and reward the dogs with quiet praise. The worst thing you can do is to constantly shout instructions to your dogs as they play. Eventually, your stream of words will blur into one. Like the birds in the trees, or the sound of the cars in the distance, your voice will become little more than background noise.

My aim here is to establish the idea that it is the dogs' role to keep up with you rather than the other way around. This is not something that has to be done constantly. Again, it is vital that the walk is as natural a process as possible for your dogs, and they are able to explore their environment freely and safely. It is a question of striking a balance. If, for instance, your dogs suddenly begin charging off in one direction, you should start walking in the opposite direction, calling the dogs' names and asking them to come as you do so. In addition to sending out a powerful message, this process introduces an element of playfulness and fun as well, and the dogs will respond to this.

One owner with pack problems whom I have helped was Pauline, a lady with a very large pack of dogs and a particularly dominant Jack Russell, called Polly. Polly lived with six other Jack Russells and two German shepherd puppies in a beautiful country house near Hinckley in Leicestershire. It was a perfect home for a large pack of dogs, as Pauline's grounds extended over twenty-two acres – more than enough room for a decent run out each day. Pauline had read my first book, but had trouble imposing herself on her dogs during the walk. When I visited her at her home, I quickly saw that the problem was Polly, who insisted on leading the other dogs in her own direction.

After working with Polly through the key stages of my method inside the house, I took her and the rest of the pack out into the grounds. They were all off-lead, and scattered to the four winds instantly. I asked Pauline to stay at the back door with me, ignoring the dogs while they did this. It did not take long for them to realise that we hadn't joined them, and they soon drifted back to the house to find out why we hadn't come with them. At this point, I called Polly to me, extending the work I had done inside the house; she was agitated, but I waited until she relaxed. Once she had calmed down and had sat patiently for a short time, the rest of the pack quickly followed suit. I then asked Pauline to join me in leading the walk.

The important lesson was that we had showed Polly who was in charge of the hunt; she understood that she had to defer to me before we went anywhere as a pack. Pauline continued working along these lines after I left. Soon after, she contacted me to tell me she had a pack of beautifully behaved dogs. An already enjoyable daily walk had turned into something to treasure.

CLOSE ENCOUNTERS: CONFRONTATIONS

It will not be long after those first, furtive steps into the world together that you and your dog will face up to your next big test: confrontations with other, less well behaved dogs. Every owner faces this moment with dread, of course. We have all been there: another dog starts barking or, worse, charging in. The situation quickly deteriorates and becomes a vicious circle: as the innocent dog sees its owner become distressed, so it retaliates. Of course, if a dog has not yet been relieved of its leadership, it will do what it can to make that threat go away. The day these confrontations cease to be a problem will be the day the world is filled with considerate and compassionate owners. And I fear that day is about as close as the day we choose a dog for Prime Minister. So, you must be prepared to deal with this situation.

Just Walk Away

I do not believe in doing anything that is alien to a dog's nature. So, once more, my philosophy for dealing with this situation is drawn from the wolf pack. The simple fact of the matter is that, in the wild, wolves avoid confrontations with other wolves at all costs. The only time they will occur is if a lone wolf tries to infiltrate a pack, or an Alpha has been lost and a new wolf makes an attempt to join the pack. These, however, are exceptional situations. For the most part, wolves are intensely territorial creatures and avoid rivalries. My advice here, then, is that you do the same.

When confronted by an aggressive or overfamiliar dog, I suggest you simply move away, cross the road or take whatever action you need to get away from the situation. You should forget about apportioning blame or feeling aggrieved at the behaviour of someone who is almost certainly less well enlightened; I do not wish to see dog dementia joining road rage as one of the sicknesses of the modern world! Just recall your dog if it is off the leash, return it to the lead and walk away, using rewards to underline the fact it has made the right decision. Of course, this is a situation that will test your leadership skills to the limit. It is why I insist that owners spend such a lengthy period of time establishing their leadership credentials at home.

This area, I admit, is one that owners sometimes question. They ask: 'What's wrong with two dogs playing with each other?' I am not for one moment suggesting that dogs should not socialise with other dogs. Far from it: as with humans, I think it's deeply unhealthy for a dog to live a solitary life away from its peers. The best comparison, again, is with a child. We all want our children to be able to play and interact with other children. But would we let them stop and play with every child they came across in the street? Would we let them go up to each child they meet and say: 'Hello, let's play'? Of course we wouldn't. I encourage all owners to allow their dog to make a circle of friends. They can be dogs you regularly meet in the park, dogs belonging to your own friends, or through dog-based social gatherings. This, of course, also allows you to meet like-minded people yourself.

Of all the cases I have dealt with over the years, that of Amber and her owner Mavis best illustrates how seriously a fear of others can affect a dog and how hard owners sometimes have to work to communicate with their dogs. As it happens, it also exemplifies the potentially tragic nonsense some so-called 'experts' present as advice.

Amber was an absolutely lovely-looking dog, a beautiful little Sheltie, or miniature 'Lassie'. Ever since Mavis had taken her in, she had shown a tendency to become hyperactive and nervous in the presence of others. At home, she would jump around the furniture when visitors entered, but the problem was at its most acute when Mavis took her out for a walk. Amber simply didn't like meeting other dogs. She would try to run off and became extremely agitated if Mavis insisted on taking her towards another dog. Rather than improving as she was exposed to more and more dogs, Amber's problem was worsening. Mavis had resorted to taking her out for walks at night and at daybreak to avoid coming across other dogs.

Mavis cared deeply about Amber and did all she could to rid her of this fear. At one point, she grew so desperate she hired the services of a so-called 'trainer' who worked with her in a park in London. He persuaded Mavis that Amber's problems could only be conquered by her confronting her fear, explaining that Amber simply had to face other dogs. I found it hard to believe this but, at one point, he actually dragged poor little Amber to meet other dogs. Of course, this only made matters worse: Amber just fell apart. She literally wet herself, and was reduced to a quivering, shaking wreck. Mavis eventually had to carry Amber home, she was so distressed, but not before her well-paid specialist had delivered his final analysis on her much-loved dog. Typically, he would not accept that he had failed and laid the blame elsewhere: 'She's too nervous because she's been badly bred,' was his dismissive verdict. If nothing else, I was determined to prove to Mavis that this man was a complete charlatan.

Mavis had become so embarrassed and concerned about Amber's behaviour at home that she had stopped having friends round to visit. When I turned up, I got an instant insight into why she had done this. Amber began bounding around the place like something out of a *Tom and Jerry* cartoon. It was clear to me that this was a particularly stressed dog and so I asked Mavis to come out of the room with me. Over a cup of tea in the kitchen, I explained the problem. Amber clearly believed she was in a position of complete power within the house. But as Mavis knew all too well, while Amber was Moby Dick at home, she was a minnow in the outside world. I set about the task of redressing the balance.

After a while, I sensed that Amber had stopped her leaping repertoire in the sitting room. I opened the door without speaking, but no sooner had I done so than she started all over again. Once more I asked Mavis to leave the room with me. A few minutes later, we returned to the sitting room and went through the same thing again. We went through this about eight times in all; Mavis' supplies of tea were severely depleted by the end of the day. Each time we left the room, the length of Amber's repertoire got shorter and shorter. Eventually, Amber showed the telltale signs of a dog that had begun to realise its situation had changed.

The key thing now was that Mavis build up on her leadership at home. My advice to her was that she did not walk Amber for ten days. She went along with this and used the time to build up her credentials as the Alpha in Amber's eyes. I'm glad to report that Mavis was rewarded with a radical change in Amber when their daily walk was resumed. Relieved of her leadership responsibilities, Amber was now able to walk down the road unthreatened. They are now able to walk about in open, wooded areas. Amber plays with dogs she regularly meets, and avoids those she doesn't without shaking, trembling and falling apart. As for Amber being badly bred, Mavis has consigned the idea to history – along with the memory of the 'expert' who suggested it.

The Pursuit of Prey: Chasing Other Animals

It is only natural that the walk is an area where many owners encounter problems with their dogs. The dog, after all, has its primal instincts are heightened for the hunt, and its adrenaline levels are soaring. A dog's nature can easily run away with it at this point, often literally. As you progress to letting your dog of the leash, this is something you must be careful to guard against.

I have dealt with many owners whose dogs chase other animals while off the leash. I have come across sheep-worriers, horse-chasers and rabbit-hunters. Each time I come across such a case, I begin by putting this behaviour in its correct context. When a dog comes across another animal, and a herbivore in particular, its instincts are to set this animal in motion and then track its movement. Because of the nature of the prey it hunts, the wolf does not attack each and every animal it comes across. To begin with, it tends to hunt large animals and thus risks picking a fight with a foe that is more than capable of beating it. As other animals also tend to move in packs, the wolf's first priority is to get its prey on the move so that it can spot its weakest links. By observing the pack in motion, the wolf will be able to tell which are the slowest, and generally most vulnerable, members. It will base its attack plans on this information. If we translate this to the dog, we can see why they tend to chase other animals. On the rare occasion when a dog actually attacks, it is probably because it has spotted a weakness in that animal.

A typical example of this was a dog, called Harley, whom I was asked to treat for my television programme. Harley was a highly excitable Samoyed who lived with his owner, Andrea, in the countryside near

155

Guildford in Surrey. Harley had several problems: in general he took absolutely no notice of Andrea. The most severe – and potentially catastrophic – problem, however, was his habit of running wild on local farms.

Harley had begun chasing cows in particular. Andrea had been visited by one local farmer who had warned her, quite rightly, that unless Harley was controlled, he would have to take drastic action. The last straw had come when Andrea had been out walking with Harley with another dog. Without any warning, Harley had suddenly frozen and then shot off like a rocket. Andrea had no idea what had caused this but when she looked into the distance she could see someone schooling a horse at the end of a lunge line. The horse was moving around in tightly reined circles. Despite the fact that the horse was three fields away, Harley had shot off in pursuit of it. It had taken all the trainer's powers to keep Harley from attacking the animal.

It was soon afterwards that I was called in. I recognised this scenario all too well – I began my first book with the story of my dog, Purdey, whose habit of chasing after animals had led to similar warnings from concerned farmers near my home many years ago. Just as I had been back then, Andrea was a responsible owner who was deeply concerned by this. She wanted to help Harley before it was too late.

I began by explaining Harley's behaviour to Andrea. In particular, I was able to put the attack on the horse into its natural context. When Harley had looked across the fields to see this horse, he had seen what looked like a horse in trouble. Why else would it be moving around in circles? That must have been a sign of weakness, perhaps a broken leg. Whatever it was, it meant that horse was easy prey – and potentially, easy meat.

Andrea grasped this idea quickly. The key thing she now needed to do was to work hard at home with Harley over the coming weeks. She had to develop Harley's abilities at the end of a lead, and then she had to begin walking him past herds of animals in the countryside.

Andrea's goal was to become such a strong and convincing leader that Harley would not even contemplate the need to go on the hunt. She had to make him so confident in her abilities that he trusted her to provide food. I warned Andrea that she had a long and difficult task ahead of her, but Harley responded well on that first afternoon. The future will be down to Andrea's determination to succeed: I'm sure she's more than up to the challenge.

TRAVELLING FURTHER AFIELD: TRAINS, PLANES AND AUTOMOBILES

I often compare learning my method with learning to drive a car. Owners progress from basics such as learning the controls to dealing with life on the open road, coping with encounters with other motorists, and so on. I often warn owners of the dangers of heading out on to the motorway when they have not learned yet to navigate their own driveway. When it comes to taking your dog out in your car, or travelling further afield by train or plane, this advice applies in the most literal sense.

Once again, it is easy to see why this area is rife with problems. When a dog jumps with its extended pack into the back of a car, or on board a plane or train, it enters an environment that is, to all intents and purposes, a miniature and mobile version of the den. When this portable den starts to move off in a way it cannot control – or even comprehend – the dog's anxieties multiply with each passing moment. Out on the road, it is assailed by sights and sounds it cannot understand or reach, and is convinced they are going to harm the pack members for which it is responsible. Is it any wonder a dog barks, leaps around and generally flips its lid when it gets into a car? For this reason, it is more imperative than ever that things are not rushed. I do not recommend that you take your dog out into the car until well into the second or even third week. Such is the level of trust required, that to do so any earlier risks your losing much of the ground you gained in the earlier stages.

I have dealt with a host of owners who have had particular problems with their dogs causing what I call 'car chaos'. The case of Ziggy illustrates where owners can typically go wrong. Ziggy's owner, Carol, was a highly successful construction industry professional from Nottingham. Ziggy was a former rescue dog, and, like so many of these dogs, he was edgy and nervous and could get extremely lively at the best of times. He used to charge at people. He was also extremely attached to Carol and would follow her everywhere. She liked to take Ziggy out and about on sites with her, but had serious trouble keeping him calm in the back of the car. Whenever Carol went anywhere near her car, Ziggy bolted towards it first. Once he was inside, he would jump around almost continuously. He would calm down when they were on motorways. But in built-up areas, when they were surrounded by other cars and pedestrians, Ziggy would bark incessantly at the outside world.

Carol read my first book and began applying my method in an attempt to rid Ziggy of all his behavioural problems. Her greatest ambition, however, was that he would be able to travel around with her. Rescue dogs, as we know, need to be treated at their own pace. They are, after all, the equivalent of children with learning disabilities, and allowances must be made. Carol had been delighted with Ziggy's response in general. He had learned to respond to her 'Thank you' at times of perceived danger, and, in the space of three weeks, he had become a much calmer dog. In the car, however, his problems remained much the same as before. It was at this stage that Carol called me in.

It did not take me long to work out where Carol had taken a wrong turn. She admitted that, while she had held back from taking Ziggy out for a walk until the second week, she had been taking him in the car from the outset. It is easy to see why Carol had done this: for a start, she did not want to be separated from the dog that she loved. And, somewhere, I'm sure she felt that her car was simply an extension of her home.

Unfortunately, her honourable motives had been totally lost on Ziggy. For all the progress Ziggy had made in the home, he had not fully accepted Carol's leadership. In addition to this, Carol was getting agitated and upset with Ziggy's behaviour in the car, so to his mind she could not successfully lead the pack within the car either. All this had become a block to his accepting her as his superior. It had also made him associate his owner's anxiety with the car – a dog is never going to think it is the cause of the problem! As a result, Ziggy was as hyperactive a passenger as ever.

When I visited Carol, I worked with Ziggy on my own to begin with. I got him to wait alongside the car, before he jumped in. It was important he begin to understand that he did not decide when he entered the car. When we went for a short drive, I simply sat beside him quietly. My message to him was that I understood and could deal with all the dangers on the other side of the car's windows. He did not need to worry; there was no requirement for him to do anything other than enjoy the scenery.

Ziggy responded well, calming down significantly, but it was up to Carol to take control of this now. She had to build up her control of their drives together, so I got her to work on different elements of it. Carol began by getting Ziggy to stay at the door of the car. He had to learn to wait for her instruction to get in. From there, he was harnessed in the back of the car. Carol then took short journeys, building up her control of him. At first, these trips were literally the length of the drive and Carol would ease the car along, silently reassuring Ziggy all the time that he was safe in her hands. When he began to calm down, she slowly lengthened the journey. Soon, Ziggy was travelling around with Carol everywhere again – only this time he was able to take in the views.

PART SIX:

DAYS 22–30

The Counter-Revolutionaries:
Leadership Challenges

By now, you should have made huge strides. You will probably be feeling pretty pleased with yourself – and rightly so. The biggest mistake you can make, however, is to imagine that it is all plain sailing from here on. Choppy, capricious and potentially disastrous waters lie ahead, and it's important to keep a firm grip on the helm.

By far the most common calls I get at this stage come from owners who suddenly find their dogs displaying strange and seemingly uncharacteristic behaviour. Typically, they call me with cries of: 'My dog has started eating the contents of the washing machine,' or, 'My dog is chasing his tail.' The phone call invariably ends with the phrase: 'He has never done this before. What on earth is this is all about?' The answer is a relatively straightforward one. Their dog is, once more, testing its owner's leadership. And, contrary to the impression the owner may have had of themselves, their dog may have decided that they are not measuring up.

At the heart of the matter are three factors that come together at the same time. Firstly, you must remember that your dog is breaking the habit of a lifetime. Until the introduction of the new regime a few weeks back, they were convinced of their status as leader. The residual memory of this lingers, particularly in homes where the dog may have ruled the roost for years. Secondly, the first weeks are, in many ways, a honeymoon period. Much like someone settling into a new school or working environment, the dog's focus and energies have been tied up in dealing with an often bewildering set of practicalities. By now it has found its feet and, as a result, is beginning to revert to its natural character once more.

The final, and most important, factor is that you will now have relaxed. Although this is understandable as the first few weeks are hard, demanding work, this is no time to rest on your laurels. Because now is the time when your dog is most likely to spot a chink in your armour.

Crime and Banishment

As you know, my method entails a quiet revolution. But what if you are dealing with a dog that is still determined to cling to power? The answer is that, sometimes, overthrowing a dictator requires more visible and stronger tactics. Again, the strongest tactic possible is drawn from the example of the wolf pack. Faced with unacceptable behaviour or insubordination in the wild, an Alpha wolf will physically eject a transgressor from the pack via aggression. The ejected wolf will be held on the outskirts of the pack until it has either learned its lesson or has left. Any attempt to reclaim its place prematurely will be met with more aggression.

At home, an owner cannot physically do this, nor should you want to. What you can do, however, is be rigid of intent and use the same principle. The more severe the challenge to your authority, the more severe your signal to the dog must be. And there is no more severe a signal than banishment from the pack. As with all the most powerful weapons, this must be used sparingly. It serves two purposes: when it is dispensed, pack members sit up and take notice, whilst the knowledge that this may happen also acts as a deterrent.

Banishment is something owners find difficult to carry out, I know, but it is vital that they remember to work with the dog's basic instincts. On the one hand, this method respects the dog's need to challenge its owner's leadership. Yet, at the same time, it uses the knowledge that a dog needs to be part of a pack environment in order to survive. These twin forces will combine to produce the right outcome.

FREQUENTLY ASKED QUESTIONS

When Do I Use Banishment?

As ever, there has to be a huge flexibility here, but I recommend it is used whenever your dog is openly defiant. If, for instance, you invite the dog to come to you and it merely looks at you and ignores the request, your dog should be cut off from you for the rest of the day. It should still be fed using gesture eating, but it should not be walked or played with, and should not even have its presence acknowledged for those twenty-four hours.

In my experience, this is often necessary with remedial dogs. They can look at you with contempt, as if to say 'Who do you think you are calling?' You have to make that dog question its decision. And the way to do this is to ignore it for a day. This may sound severe, but a way is needed to transmit your message, and what are the alternatives? The old-fashioned method would have been to shout and holler and shake the dog. How much of that is going to mean anything to it? Isn't it far better to use a language it understands and threaten it with a sanction that really impinges on its quality of life?

What If My Dog Really Misbehaves?

In really extreme cases, I ask owners to ignore their dogs for two, three or even four days. This happened to me once with my own much-loved dog, Sasha. At the time my springer, Molly, was coming into season, so it was a time of heightened tension within any pack. One day, as Molly walked past, Sasha grabbed at her in a violent way and a brief confrontation ensued.

Such times are testing for any leader. It is imperative that a show of strength is made – and that it is one that the dog understands. I was not going to have behaviour of this kind in my pack so I drilled Sasha back under the table, using my eyes alone. I didn't speak a word but she knew I wasn't happy with her. I then decided I was going to keep her there for two hours. So I stayed in the kitchen, clearing out cupboards. Every time Sasha attempted to move out from under that table, I glared at her and she went back. She knew she was in trouble, and knew that her leader was in charge. After two hours I decided to let her out, but again I did this without looking at her or speaking to her. When she made a move to go out, I let her go. She crept out, then came to my side, trying to apologise. I ignored her and continued to ignore her for four days. I showed her this was totally unacceptable.

During this time, I took Sasha out for walks with the others, but I kept her out of the group again using my eyes. Whenever she tried to rejoin the pack, I kept her out with a glare. This was no easy thing to do – I found it as hard as any owner could have done. I loved my dogs and I wanted them to be happy together as a pack. But at the same time I did not want my dogs to fight, and this was the only way of ensuring they didn't. Ultimately, the ends justified the means. After four days, I welcomed Sasha back into the pack and there was no more trouble between her and Molly. The message had been a hard one, but it had got through.

Challenges to leadership can manifest themselves in all manner of ways, as two examples from my casebook may help illustrate. The first involved a family with three dogs: Stan, Ollie and Buster. This trio lived with their owner, Denise, in Peterborough. They had made great progress in applying my method: the dogs behaved very well at home, gesture eating had been successful, so was reuniting after a separation. The dogs' repertoire had reduced to such an extent that the five-minute rule had evolved into the one-minute rule. The only problem lay on the walk, when the dogs continued to pull on the lead and charged into a boundary fence as strangers passed by. Debbie, like so many owners I meet, was determined to iron out this last, frustrating problem. She needed a helping hand with the final phase, and so requested my help.

Time and again, I arrive in these situations to discover that the problem area has arisen outside of the home. This is understandable: we all feel far more in control within the confines of our own home. Outside, in a world full of unpredictability, our confidence levels are diminished. Unfortunately, this is something a dog seizes on instinctively. It was clear to me that all three dogs were not yet fully convinced of Debbie's leadership credentials. But it was Buster who demonstrated his doubts in the most memorable – and amusing – way.

Debbie had made one classic mistake. Because Buster was smaller than the other two dogs, she had imagined his problems were smaller. Buster is what I jokingly call a 'multi-pedigreed' dog. As a result, Debbie had concentrated on her Labradors more than on him. She had thought Buster would require less effort; how wrong she had been!

Until now, the dogs had shown every other sign of believing in Debbie's leadership. It was when I appeared on the scene that Buster really showed the true nature of his feelings, and staged his last stand. Debbie and I sat in a conservatory, where Stan and Ollie, the two Labradors, were fine. Buster, however, was trotting around the place, looking very preoccupied with things. As I sat and listened to Debbie's account of the situation, studiously ignoring all his posturing, Buster started barking at me. Debbie immediately came out with the line: 'He doesn't normally do that.' I got her to lead him outside the conservatory to the garden. Out of the corner of our eyes, we watched Buster do a circuit of the garden. He came up to the glass, barked, then calmed down again.

When we let Buster in, he scampered over to a favourite wicker chair and was calm there for a short while. Then, suddenly, he started pawing rhythmically away at a cushion. Again, Debbie was bemused: 'He's never done that before either.' His barking had failed so, clearly, Buster was going to try something else.

Once more, Buster was exiled from the conservatory. And once more he went off to do a circuit of the garden, clearly planning his next move. We soon found out what that was. The next time he was let back in, he darted behind some of the large plants Debbie had kept there. For a few moments, all was peace and quiet. Then, as if in slow motion, Debbie and

I saw one of the plant pots moving ever so slowly and slightly. When we looked a little closer, we saw that Buster was there chewing furiously at one of Debbie's precious plants. I must admit we had both found Buster's previous attempts to assert himself funny. This time we couldn't hold back and both let out a giggle.

Buster was telling Debbie that, for all the progress she had made, he still didn't accept her as leader. Dogs are sensitive, and Debbie confirmed to me that she didn't really see herself as an authoritative leader. This was the key: her belief level was not high enough, therefore the dog's belief level was not high enough either.

Eventually, Debbie prevailed through showing strong, silent leadership, and Buster gave up. Within a few days, by going back to basics with the principles of Amichien Bonding, he, like Stan and Ollie, had accepted the new order. The conservatory had been Buster's Little Bighorn, the site of his brave, but futile, last stand.

A dog can show it is unconvinced about leadership in a variety of ways. Another owner I visited was completely baffled by her dog, Danny's, behaviour. The owner, Sarah, was three-and-a-half weeks into applying my method on Danny, her terrier. Until then, things had gone along a predictable, successful course. In the home, in particular, Danny had responded encouragingly. His only weakness came when people passed outside his front window. He would leap on to a chair and then on to the windowsill. Sarah had no ornaments left there, so animated were Danny's protests at passers-by. Even here, however, his behaviour was improving. His protests were becoming less dramatic and shorter in length.

Then one day, as Sarah played with Danny and a toy in the garden, he did something he had never done before. When she threw him the ball with a bell inside it, Danny took it and ran into a corner where he proceeded to shred it. There was a manic energy about him, it was, Sarah said, as if he was very, very angry with her. She rang me for help.

I recognised Danny's case as a classic example of a dog coming back at its owner and mounting a serious challenge to their leadership. I explained to Sarah that, effectively, Danny was saying: 'You have applied for the job of leader, and I have agreed that you can have it. But now you are not measuring up to the challenge. And that is really annoying me.'

Sarah clearly had to regain the upper hand here as quickly as possible. I got her to remove all the toys from the garden and stop playing with Danny for a few days. He was very angry with her because, when Sarah had resumed normal play after a few days, he had once more shredded a plastic toy. While this was going on, I got Sarah to reintroduce gesture eating and to become more formal in her dealings with Danny once more. Within three weeks he had become calm once more. The counter-revolution had been quelled, and Sarah was determined that Danny would have a leader he could trust in the future.

A dog has no understanding of human status: it is of no relevance to it that its owner is a celebrity or a supermarket shelf-stacker, a president or a postman. A dog judges its leader by their ability to lead convincingly, and you cannot con a dog into believing this if it is not true. If there is a weakness, the dog will latch on to it. As a footnote to this section, it is worth mentioning the example of a dog that had its own small place in the history of the twentieth century. As a young girl, I can remember seeing footage of Adolf Hitler with his pet German shepherd. The two were playing at his Bavarian retreat. At the time, of course, I had no real understanding of Hitler or his significance in the world; my main interest was dogs. What struck me about what I saw was how unhappy his dog appeared.

On the several occasions I have seen the footage since, I have felt exactly the same thing. I now know the monstrous truth about Hitler. And I know how, through fear and intimidation, he prevented anyone from challenging his leadership. Few humans found themselves able to stand up to his overwhelming, bullying personality. I'm sure he treated his shepherd with the same arrogant imperious manner. Yet the dog was having none of it. Hitler hadn't even begun to convince him he was a real leader. I wonder what inner weaknesses the dog sensed in him?

ALL CHANGE: COPING WITH UPHEAVAL

There will, of course, be times when your family's shape and surroundings change: children may grow up and leave home, family members may pass away, partners may separate. This may easily unsettle and upset a dog. Equally, your family may face the upheaval of moving home. The prospect of adapting to new surroundings will be as challenging to the family pet as it is to everyone else.

It is easy to see why such moments can throw a dog off kilter. Dogs equate change with a challenge to the existing order and need to see order restored as quickly and emphatically as possible. So, in each of these circumstances, the key is to remain calm yourself, and to remain the inspiring, reliable leader your dog has grown to believe in. If the change of scenery or personnel causes major behavioural problems in your dog, revert to the early days of the Amichien Bonding process, reintroducing gesture eating and cutting out walks until your dog has once more accepted its status within the home. As with so many aspects of applying my method, it is a case of using patience, understanding and plain common sense.

Long Separations

At the opposite end of the scale from the normal, day-to-day separations I have dealt with in the earlier section of this book, are the lengthy separations that come when you take long holidays or travel on extended business trips. Anxious owners naturally worry about leaving their pets for long periods of time, fearing that the separation may affect their relationship somehow. In my experience, there is little to worry about. In fact, as I have already explained, a dog has no sense of time so will not differentiate in any significant way between an absence of a few hours or a few weeks. In both instances, the important thing is that the dog re-establishes itself in the home and that you reassert your leadership immediately on your return.

New Arrivals

Nothing creates a more joyous transformation within the home than the arrival of a new baby. New parents often worry about the effect the newborn family member will have on their pets. The fact is there is no reason why it should have any real impact at all, other than a happy one. A dog that has been relieved of the pressure of leadership will take its lead from you. It will, naturally, have its curiosity aroused by the demanding – and occasionally deafening – new arrival. You must deal with this in the way you now deal with all unexpected noises: by thanking the dog for its interest and taking charge of the situation yourself. As ever, the key is not to make a huge commotion.

As a cautionary tale, I will mention one family who, unintentionally, made matters worse rather than better. Craig had spent six years living with his dog, Joe, before he met and had a child with his girlfriend. When the baby arrived home for the first time, the couple did what most sensible parents do – they made a big fuss of Joe, the older 'child' in the home. Their intentions were, of course, entirely honourable; they did not want him to feel left out or overshadowed by his new 'sibling'. The problem was that, in this case, they were doing the exact opposite of what they should. Joe already believed he was the leader of the house. By their behaviour, the family was vesting even greater power in him.

The baby was six months old when I was called in to see Joe. Joe's stress levels by then were so high, I was seriously worried that he was going to have a heart attack. Joe put up a huge battle before relinquishing his leadership. His repertoire went on for three-and-a-half hours, the longest I have ever known. I explained to the couple why Joe was unable to cope with these altered family circumstances. Craig and his family understood and began to implement my method. When I last spoke to them, they were still struggling but their resolve was strong. I'm sure they will get there in the end.

PART SEVEN:
DAY 31 ONWARDS ...

Keep an Open Mind

If I have learned anything in the years that I have been working with dogs, it is to expect the unexpected. It is, if I am honest, the most enjoyable element of my work. From the tail-chasers and paw-chewers, to the dogs with phobias about phones and fireworks, I have relished meeting each challenge. No two days can ever be the same – nor would I want them to be. There is, however, a common quality that is shared by all the owners I meet: all of them care deeply for their dogs. And all of them are prepared to go that extra mile to give those dogs a better life.

The method I have outlined in this book will provide every owner with the foundations upon which to communicate with their dog. But real, lasting success will come to those who add some of the other, almost instinctive, qualities that I have seen demonstrated over the years. They are not special gifts in any sense – anyone can have them. You should aspire to include these qualities too. If you do, I feel sure you will enjoy an even richer and more rewarding life with your dog.

I like to believe that my ability to keep an open mind has brought me a long way in my dealings with dogs. If I had been closed to new and original ways of thinking – no matter how extreme or far-fetched, at times – I would not have made the breakthroughs that underpin my work. It is an attitude that I believe can serve all dog owners.

A case I dealt with a year or so ago is an interesting case in point. I was asked to visit a family of five who owned a lively dog. The family had been applying my method and had made tremendous progress. The problem centred on the family's teenage daughter. The dog had been with them since it was eight months old. It was extremely well behaved – so much so that, when I arrived, I wondered whether there was very much for me to do. But then the daughter arrived and everything changed. The dog backed away and ran into the kitchen, where he cowered in a corner, trembling.

The mind works overtime in situations like this. 'What on earth had this girl done to the dog to produce this sort of reaction?' I asked myself. In other circumstances there may have been cause for concern. I might have wondered whether there had been some abuse going on here. But there was no question of the girl having been unkind to the dog: she simply thought the dog hated her.

It was as I spoke to the girl that I was struck by the perfume she was wearing. It was not overly strong but, equally, it was hard to miss at close range. To a dog, such smells are deeply confusing. It knows the aromas of its pack members and associates strongly with these. Could it be that, since the daughter had started wearing perfume, like any average teenager, the dog's attitude towards her had changed? I had to tread carefully here, so I asked the girl whether she always wore the perfume. She was slightly offended by the question but eventually understood why I had enquired. I asked her to stop wearing it around the house for a week, and also asked her to stop using perfumed soap. Within two weeks the dog was reacting to her in exactly the same way as he reacted to the rest of the family. She did not smell any less delightful when she went out at night.

Be Adaptable

Most of the dog owners I meet are committed, caring people who put the welfare of their animals at the top of their priorities. They will do anything to ensure their dog lives a happy and fulfilled life. Unfortunately, however, the world is not a straightforward place, and there are obstacles that sometimes cannot be overcome. It is important that, for this reason, you are able to adapt to the surroundings around you. And sometimes that involves making allowances for those people who do not share our view of the world.

When I think about this aspect of dog ownership, I often recollect the determination of Linda, a nurse from Yorkshire. Linda lived with her two Cairn terriers, Milly and Molly. Unfortunately, her next door neighbour was the owner of a very badly behaved and aggressive dog, and could not have been further removed from the kind of caring dog owner that Linda represented. The neighbour's dog would bark at Milly and Molly, and would fling itself in a rage against the fence that separated the two gardens. Milly and Molly would react to this aggression, and the noise the three dogs made would be deafening.

We can no more protect ourselves from such undesirable neighbours than we can from the onset of the seasons every year: it is a part of life. It was clear this was not an environment that was going to allow Linda a completely free run with her dogs. By adopting an adaptable approach, however, she performed minor miracles. She began by erecting a formidable, six-foot fence between her and the garden next door. She then set about introducing my method to her dogs, concentrating her work inside the home. When it came to the time to take her dogs into the garden, she combined the work she had done on perceived danger and the come and recall to good effect. When the dog next door began his barking, she called Milly and Molly to her, rewarded them with tidbits and thanked them for alerting her to the danger.

By teaching Milly and Molly to believe in her leadership absolutely, she soon persuaded them to ignore the dog next door completely; gradually his charges and protests became less intense. This dog was very unhappy. The more Milly and Molly had reacted to him, the more animated he became. Denied any interaction, he eventually gave up. I like to think we helped him indirectly too.

Fortunately, this story has an even happier ending. A few months after I met her, Linda got another job in another part of Yorkshire. She was delighted to find a house only three doors away from her brother. It was hardly surprising that the dogs' behaviour changed almost immediately. Linda described them as transformed, joyful creatures. In stark contrast to her previous neighbour, the people in the two houses separating her from her brother happily allowed them to build a channel which allowed the dogs to run from one house to the other. I like to think someone, somewhere was rewarding Linda for her perseverance...

Think Holistically: See the Big Picture

The most common misconception I come across among owners of multiple packs is the idea that the problems of one dog can be treated in isolation. This is simply impossible: the pack must be treated as a whole, for a variety of reasons – not least the fact that far too often the owner is guilty of mistaken identity. I often come across cases where the root cause of the pack's problem does not lie with the dog they imagine, but elsewhere.

So it proved in one particular case I was called in to deal with, that of the dogs I refer to as Puppy X and his uncle. This was another of the MI5-style operations I have been involved in. Once more, I had been sworn to secrecy on the case by the client. And once more the client came from the world of breeding and show dogs.

The family concerned were the owners of a large, and very successful, show kennel. They asked me to tackle a problem with one of the thirteen dogs they had at the time, an eighteen-month-old dog. The family had a long and well-regarded record at dog shows. As a youngster of six or nine months, the puppy had done well in the show arena. Now, at the age of eighteen months, however, his demeanour was totally different. The dog would back off from judges whenever they approached him. Sometimes he would sink down on his haunches. The owners told me their dog had become really unhappy, and as genuine dog lovers they could not countenance this.

This behaviour in dogs is far from uncommon within the show world, particularly if the owners grow anxious and frustrated within the ring. This nervousness can transmit itself to the dog – with predictable consequences. This was patently not the case with these owners, as they quite rightly regarded their dog's welfare as far more important than a winner's rosette. They told me when I got there: 'It won't bother us if he doesn't go to another dog show in his life, we just want him to be happy.'

I arrived at their property and was led into a room where three dogs were waiting. It was fairly obvious which one I had been called to deal with. Puppy X's demeanour was very defensive and he was edging towards a comfortable-looking cage in the corner. Clearly this was his own space, his personal den. But it was not long either before I had spotted that the cause of the puppy's anxiety was also in the room. And that was his four-year-old uncle.

I had gone into the house in my usual manner, refusing to engage with or acknowledge the dogs there in any way. While the youngest dog cowered and the second dog, clearly the mother of the pack, just stared at me, the uncle could not cope with my presence and went into an extraordinary repertoire of barking and jumping. The more he protested, the more I made a point of ignoring him. It was as if he was saying: 'Who does she think she is?'

What was really revealing was the way in which the uncle treated his owners. As his repertoire continued, he jumped up onto the knee of the father of the household. I asked the owner to repel the dog, but he found it difficult because the dog's anxiety levels were so high. It was clear to me then why Puppy X was not performing well within the show ring. Quite simply, the dog had little or no regard for its owners because of their status within the home. There was only one leader there – and it was not the owners, it was the uncle. I had no doubt that the jumping up I had seen was a regular event. And that, until now, the uncle had got exactly what he wanted from his owners.

I explained my analysis of the situation to the family. And I told them that, rather than tackling the younger dog, my job would begin with the uncle. I worked with the three dogs that were in the room to begin with. Eventually, the uncle's repertoire came to an end; it must have taken about half an hour of over-the-top behaviour before he gave up. He was obviously a highly intelligent dog, but he was soon coming to me.

While the uncle had been going through this process, Puppy X had remained in his own space. It was clear he was wary of getting involved. But it was also obvious that he was waiting to see how events panned out. When, eventually, the uncle calmed down and began responding to my requests to come, Puppy X slowly inched his way forward. Seeing his uncle responding gave the younger dog encouragement. And for the first time he, too, began to come towards me. He had sensed a change in the household's hierarchy and was reacting to it.

My next task was to introduce the rest of the pack to the method. I began by asking the owners to bring in the two puppies. The moment they reappeared, the uncle went into his repertoire once more while, at the same time, the younger dog retreated to his cage. I waited for the uncle to calm down once more before getting the puppies to come to me. This was – as is often the case with packs – a long and laborious process. Owners often feel they are taking one step forwards and one step back, but in fact they are always moving on.

I could not work my way through the entire pack in one sitting. Besides, the owners told me there were clear groupings within the pack, so I emphasised the need to work with these mini packs separately and left them to it. The owners grasped the principles immediately. They worked hard over the coming weeks, and were rewarded with huge improvements in their pack's behaviour. Puppy X lost his haunted look within three days. Within the canine hierarchy, the uncle remained top dog but, when it came to his human owners, he had relinquished responsibility. And that was a relief to everyone.

Perseverance Pays

We are all assailed by self-doubt now and again. If ever I question the worth of the work I am doing, I think of some of the hundreds of success stories with which I have now been associated, either directly or indirectly. One of the most heart-warming of these provides a perfect illustration of the importance of perseverance, and not giving up on a dog.

The story was told to me by a Customs Squad dog handler, who approached me and introduced himself at Cruft's this year. He explained that he had been using my method in his work with a rescued spaniel being trained as a sniffer dog. Customs call these dogs 'second chancers' because they have – somehow – lost their first chance and ended up in the rescue centre. The Customs and Excise Squad offer them a second opportunity. For many dogs, it might be their last.

It looked like this spaniel had also blown his second chance. He had been earmarked for work at Dover docks, where he would search for drugs and contraband, but he had quickly proven too hyperactive to concentrate on the task at hand. When let loose in a cargo container or the back of a haulage truck, the dog would skitter around in a haphazard fashion, sniffing in one corner at one moment, then the other corner the next. There was no method to his madness at all, and this was clearly not going to be accepted within the professional environment of the Customs and Excise squad.

Again, this behaviour was no real surprise given the dog's background. Fortunately for him, he had found a handler who was willing to go that extra mile. The handler told me that he had applied the method from my first book. The primary example of a rescue dog there was of my Jack Russell, Barmie. The slow, patient approach I was required to take in restoring Barmie's confidence in humans had provided a blueprint for the handler during his first few weeks with this dog. His patience and perseverance had soon paid off. Within a few weeks, he was working with a completely different dog. Rather than leaping around all over the place, the spaniel had become much more methodical. He would work his way through the boxes, sniffing them out thoroughly before moving on to the next one; there was nothing random about his work any more.

The handler's hard work quickly paid spectacular dividends. Soon after he had been put to work at Dover, the dog boarded a large lorry recently arrived in England from the Continent. The old dog would have bounded around haphazardly. Now it worked its way through the cargo, until its attention was drawn by a particular package. As he became more animated his handler moved in. The dog had hit the jackpot: the lorry contained heroin worth half a million pounds. It was one of the biggest drug busts of the year. He had earned his second chance – in some style.

In the course of my work, I am asked to deal with a variety of dogs – from the aggressive and overexcitable to the sensitive and nervous. When it comes to helping them and their owners overcome their difficulties, I treat all of them as equals. Occasionally, however, I come across cases that push me, my method and the owner concerned to the outer limits. To borrow a phrase from George Orwell, some dogs are – in terms of a challenge – more equal than others.

None of the diverse collection of dogs I have encountered was more equal than the pet that became known as 'Damien, the Devil Dog'. He represented perhaps the toughest test any owner has faced using my method. And the way in which that owner overcame the challenge should offer solace to anyone who finds themselves struggling to implement my ideas.

To protect the privacy of its owner, I will refer to this dog, a Welsh springer, as Tim. Tim displayed many of the common problems found in dogs: what distinguished him was that he was extreme in all of them. He pulled on the lead for all he was worth; he reacted to the arrival of the morning post by ripping it up; his aggressive streak was so bad that he had to be muzzled when visiting the vet. Tim's behaviour had driven a wedge between Jenny, his owner, and her family. She was married with grown-up daughters, and the rest of the family were agreed that the dog had to go. Jenny had tried all she could to improve his behaviour, but nothing had worked.

Every now and again, I come across a dog that has the look of a natural Alpha, the sort of animal that, cast into the wild environment, would rise without any challenge to the top of its pack. Tim was one of these dogs. He was not that big – he didn't weigh more than 50lbs – but he had immense presence. Jenny, in comparison, was a very gentle lady. It was easy to see why the hierarchy had established itself in the way it had.

Despite the daunting task ahead, Jenny was absolutely determined to help Tim. I was very touched when I first spoke to her. 'How can I let him go – where would I put him?' she asked me plaintively. The dice were loaded against her in many ways. In asking people to adopt my method, I am asking them to take a leap of faith. They must believe – no matter how improbable it may seem – that by applying my principles, their dog's behaviour will improve. Unfortunately, Jenny's family were unwilling to share her faith. Her husband wanted Tim's behaviour to improve too but he simply could not see that adopting my method was going to help. In effect, Jenny was on her own.

As I have stressed throughout this book, there can be no precise timetable of events to my method. A lot of people want to wave a magic wand and have the problems disappear overnight: life does not work that way. Yes, some dogs relinquish their leadership with barely a protest. But others fight tooth and nail to cling on to a status they believe to be rightfully theirs. No dog ever put up a fight to compare with Tim.

Jenny began applying the four elements of Amichien Bonding in the normal way. It was clear from the beginning that Tim was not going to give in. Any ideas Jenny had of heading out for a walk after one week were quickly forgotten. It was only after two weeks of working with Tim that she saw her first sign of progress: he had begun calming down during his repertoire. A week after that, Tim came to Jenny when she asked him to – something that had never happened in the house before. Until then, Tim had looked at the humans in the house as if they were total idiots.

Progress was, however, painfully slow. Jenny often felt that, for every step forward, she was taking two back. Soon after she had begun to get Tim to come to her, he began rebelling. He would run upstairs and pull all her shoes out of the bedroom wardrobe. She had to put a gate there to stop him trashing the room. To be fair to Jenny, the situation was not helped by the fact that the rest of the family were not applying the method. She was also a lady with a lot of self-doubt and, quite simply, Tim had not even begun to be convinced by her leadership. The pressure this was putting on Jenny was considerable. And at times, inevitably, she cracked. She would phone me every now and then in a terribly distressed state; she would cry and sob down the phone. Sometimes we would talk about Tim for an hour.

This struggle went on for two months before it entered its next phase. By this point, Jenny hadn't even progressed to taking Tim out for a walk, and he had shown signs of tightening rather than loosening his grip on the leadership of the pack. One day when Jenny invited Tim to come, he simply turned his back on her. She rang me almost immediately, once more distraught at his defiance. My message to her at this point was simple: this is a battle of wills, and your will must be stronger. 'If the dog ignores you, then you must totally ignore it – for a whole day.'

So, the next day, Jenny ignored Tim completely. Her only contact with him was at mealtimes, when she gesture ate in front of him. When, the following day, she once more tried to get Tim to come and he turned his back on her again, she responded by ignoring him for the next two days. This process went on until Jenny ignored him for six whole days. There was no aggression or anger in her body language. She simply got on with her day-to-day life without acknowledging the dog in any way, shape or form.

The reaction of Jenny's family and friends to this was predictable. They thought she was crazy. Some told her she was being cruel to the dog; others suggested she simply give the dog 'a good hiding'; choke chains and even an electric collar were suggested. Jenny, to her credit, refused to quit, however. And she was rewarded almost immediately after that six-day stand-off came to an end.

The next day, Jenny called Tim to her and, rather than turning his back again, he moved – very slowly and gingerly – towards her. It didn't seem like much of a breakthrough, but, in the context of the war, it was a significant battle won. Until now, Tim had always had Jenny dancing to his tune. Now she had the upper hand – and it was vital that she did not lose it.

About an hour after this had happened, Jenny asked him to come again and he refused. She called me immediately: 'What's happening here?' she asked. 'He's still testing you,' I told her. 'Be firm.' Jenny's response was to return to ignoring Tim completely, this time for four days. It was not as severe a consequence as the previous time because Tim had made a small move in the right direction. If he was a smart dog – and there was no question in either of our minds that he was – Tim would understand this and react accordingly.

Sure enough, when Jenny called Tim at the end of the four days, Tim came to her readily. Now I asked Jenny to really capitalise on her gains. Rather than rewarding Tim with some attention, I asked her to ignore him for a day. Jenny, of course, thought this was harsh, but I explained that she had to ram home the message that she was the leader. And now was the time to do it.

The morning after she had ignored him for the whole day, Tim came readily to Jenny the moment she called him. I asked her to leave him then and call him again in the afternoon. Again he came. Over the next three days, I asked her to gradually build on this, calling Tim one more time each day. By the end of the fourth day she had called him four times – and he had come every time. She was even gently stroking his head as a means of praise.

Four months after she had begun the process, the turnaround had finally begun. Tim had at last begun to accept that Jenny was, after all, a formidable leader – someone worthy of respect, and someone he would be prepared to follow. I must admit it felt very odd when Jenny stopped calling me shortly afterwards. I'd grown so used to hearing her voice at the end of the telephone. Almost every day I was tempted to call her, but I knew I had to leave her to build on this success. It was five more weeks before I heard from her again. She couldn't mask her excitement as she delivered her opening words. 'The devil dog is no more!'

At first, even I was sceptical. I was waiting for Jenny to tell me that he'd been behaving well for a day. It turned out that, for the past week, Tim had transformed into a lovely dog. He had been out on a walk each day and had behaved impeccably every step of the way, every day. He had responded to Jenny's quiet 'Thank you' when anyone came to the door. He had even been for a booster jab at the vet, and there had been no need for a muzzle. Jenny's family were, predictably, astonished. Equally predictably, they were now once more showing interest in Tim.

This is proof of what can be achieved through a combination of perseverance, self-belief and faith. I felt proud that I had been able to help someone through such a tough process and, most of all, I felt proud of Jenny. I hope she provides a lesson to us all.

Be Realistic

Some things are beyond us. We cannot keep our dogs alive forever; we cannot force the rest of the world to share our feelings for them. We have to be realistic about these things. On a personal level, every owner must accept what is practically possible. This is not always easy, but it must be faced. It was something I had to accept myself as I tried to heal the wounds inflicted on my own pack in May 2001.

In the weeks that followed the tragic losses of Sasha and Barmie, I had steadily restored my own status within my pack. But there was no escaping the fact that the rivalry that had erupted between Ceri and Molly had solidified into something lasting. Much as I would have loved to put the clock back, I could not.

By applying my method I was able to ensure that, when I was around, there was harmony: I was able to nip any hint of aggression between the two in the bud. My problem, however, was that my work was keeping me away from my pack for extended periods. I was travelling overseas and working on a television series; I was simply not as visible a presence in the home as I had been before. And this was where I had to face up to the hard facts of life myself. I knew this was only going to be a temporary situation. But I had to reflect the reality: I was their leader and my absence was going to have repercussions.

After much soul-searching, I came to the conclusion that, for the time being at least, Molly and Ceri had to lead separate lives. This is not to say that I ruled out a reconciliation in the future. I have seen so many remarkable things within the dog world that I would never rule anything out. Yet, realistically, I knew that in the short term they would only inflict damage on each other, and on the pack as a whole, if they were together. I had seen it happen once, and I was not going to watch it happening again.

The kindest way of dividing them was along bloodlines. So I kept Molly and Ceri with their immediate families, segregated in different areas of my home. I allowed the junior members of these mini packs to mix freely. Sadie, too, was free to spend time with each grouping as she pleased. In the main, however, Molly and Ceri were kept apart. The only concession here was during the walk when we were able to take both dogs out, but only with each constantly on a lead and under the control of different handlers. This upset me greatly: prior to Sasha's death, I had been able to go out on my own, walking with my pack together as one – it was a source of great pride to me. Now they had, in effect, become separate units. As time wore on, however, this decision helped us all get back to some semblance of normality.

Time is, of course, the great healer. At the time of writing, our lives together have returned to something approaching the happy harmony of old. Ceri and Molly have come to an accommodation. They can accept being in the same room together and their ease in each other's company is growing slowly but steadily. I know it will take only the slightest incident to unravel all this, so I watch them like a hawk when they are together. Mercifully, there have been no repeats of the awful, upsetting violence of the past. Throughout this book, I have preached the importance of persistence, hard work and understanding. In the days, weeks and months ahead, I know that I, too, will have to continue displaying these qualities. I am strengthened by two certainties, however: I know that we will find a way of living together, and I know, too, that it will be my dogs that will lead the way.

EPILOGUE

Speaking Canine

I have spent the last decade attempting to learn a language that, I believe, is universally understood by dogs. During this time I have, predictably, encountered those who are simply unwilling to entertain that such a thing is even possible. Fortunately I was prepared for this by my mentor, Monty Roberts. In the foreword to my first book, he cautioned me against what he called, 'human nature's almost limitless capacity for negativity'. How wise those words now seem. Yet, every now and again, I experience something so powerful that it re-energises me and makes me want to press on further. Such an experience came in Poland.

If I ever doubted how much we stand to gain by making the effort to understand and communicate in ways outside our normal experience, Poland put me right from the moment I got off the plane. I had been determined to learn at least a few phrases in the local language. So I learned to say *Dzięckuję* (thank you) and *Dzieńdobry* (hello). The smiles that spread across my hosts' faces whenever I dipped into my limited vocabulary were generous ones. So often English-speaking travellers in particular assume the world understands them; it is simply bad manners in my view. As I travelled around Poland, people seemed genuinely touched by my clumsy linguistic efforts. I'm sure the welcome I received, and the reception my ideas were given, were more positive as a result.

Of course my argument is that, when it comes to dogs, all human languages are identical: whether we speak in Polish or Cantonese, our dogs do not understand a word. What they do understand, however, is the language of the pack, which I sometimes now refer to as 'Canine'. I was reminded of just how misguided some people can be on this issue when I recently worked with a Rottweiler that was causing its new owners problems. The previous owner had been Swedish, and the new owners had even gone to the trouble of advertising on local radio and TV for someone to teach them to speak the language they believed their dog understood.

It was during my trip to Poland that I was provided with my most significant moment on this matter. I was staying with a lovely couple, Miroslav and Anna, just outside Warsaw. They bred Corgis – very successfully I might add. In the evening I was sitting in their living room with them, relaxing after a busy day, when one of them came into the room. The dog was called Kiss, an American-bred bitch and champion within the Polish show world. Without any great fuss, Kiss padded along and jumped up on to the sofa next to me. Anna was surprised: 'She doesn't do that,' she said, a puzzled expression on her face. 'She always runs away from strangers.'

We carried on talking. I was off duty, so I didn't ask whether they had any particular problems with their dogs – they seemed more than happy with them. It was a few minutes later that Kiss scampered off into a corner for a drink. When she'd finished, she looked up at me. I just smiled at her and softly invited her to come. She came straight to me and resumed her position next to me for a cuddle. Miroslav and Anna couldn't believe it, but my explanation to them was simple. Since I'd arrived in the house I'd demonstrated that I was someone to be trusted – not feared.

Our conversation was in English, which they both spoke well. It occurred to me afterwards what a significant moment this was in its own small way. It was the first time I'd seen my method work in such an unfamiliar environment. It reminded me why I'd begun my journey ten years ago. And it strengthened my resolve to continue along the road to understanding this language more fully. I joked with Miroslav and Anna that pleasant evening, saying: 'I'm afraid my Polish isn't up to much. But my Canine – that's coming along pretty well!' Here's to a world in which everyone learns to speak the language of man's best friend.

Index

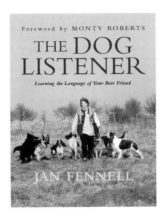

THE DOG LISTENER
by JAN FENNELL

This is the best-selling book that brought Jan's remarkable gifts to thousands of grateful dog owners the world over. Her unique understanding of the canine world and its instinctive language made Jan a household name by showing how to bring the most delinquent of dogs to heel.

This easy-to-follow guide to understanding Jan's simple techniques draws on her countless case histories of problem dogs – from biters and barkers to bicycle chasers – to show how we can bridge the language barrier that separates man from his best friend.

In *The Dog Listener* Jan shares her secrets, telling us how she grew determined to find a more compassionate alternative to standard 'obedience' training techniques and, ultimately, how to communicate with canines.

ISBN 0-00-257204-4